𝔇𝔢𝔞𝔯 𝔈𝔞𝔤𝔩𝔢

The Civil War Correspondence

of Stephen H. Bogardus, Jr.

to the

𝔓𝔬𝔲𝔤𝔥𝔨𝔢𝔢𝔭𝔰𝔦𝔢 𝔇𝔞𝔦𝔩𝔶 𝔈𝔞𝔤𝔩𝔢

The Scuppernong Press

DEAR EAGLE:
THE CIVIL WAR CORRESPONDENCE
OF STEPHEN H. BOGARDUS, JR.
© 2004 Joel Craig

The Scuppernong Press, Wake Forest, NC, USA
All rights reserved. Printed in the United States of America.

No part of this book maybe reproduced or transmitted in any form or by any means, electronic or mechanical, including photocopying, recording, or by any information and storage and retrieval system, without written permission from the publisher.

Library of Congress Cataloging-in-Publication Data

Bogardus, Stephen H., 1838-1907.
Dear Eagle: the Civil War correspondence of Stephen H. Bogardus, Jr. to the Poughkeepsie Daily Eagle /[edited by Joel Gregory Craig].—
1st trade paperback ed. p. cm.
ISBN 0-9701726-2-1 (pbk. : alk. paper)
1. Bogardus, Stephen H., 1838-1907—Correspondence. 2. United States. Army. New York Infantry Regiment, 5th (1861-1863) 3. New York (State)—History—Civil War, 1861-1865—Personal narratives. 4. United States—History—Civil War, 1861-1865—Personal narratives. 5. Soldiers—New York (State)—Poughkeepsie—Correspondence. 6. Poughkeepsie (N.Y.)—Biography. I. Craig, Joel Gregory, 1961- II. Poughkeepsie Eagle (Poughkeepsie, N.Y. : 1850) III. Title.
E523.5 5th .B64 2002
973.7'447—dc212002002111

Dedicated to the men of Dutchess County
who served with the 5th New York Duryée Zouaves.

Poughkeepsie Boys, Huzzah!

Acknowledgements

    I would like to acknowledge those who assisted in this project and offer my sincere thanks for their contributions. I am greatly indebted to my parents for encouraging my interest in history and to my family for patiently enduring my obsession with people and events that happened more than a century ago. My sincere thanks to Clarence Anspake of Bellmore, New York, for information on Bogardus' genealogy; the staff at Adriance Memorial Library, Poughkeepsie, New York, for their assistance; and Jeremy and Heather Harvey of Alexandria, Virginia, for their photographic contributions. I would especially like to thank Brian Pohanka for his encouragement and his generous donation of both time and material.

Foreword

"I am no writer," Stephen H. Bogardus, Jr. noted in one of his wartime letters. "Nothing but a soldier fighting for his country's honor." But as this volume so clearly attests, the young New Yorker was in fact skilled with the pen as well as the sword. Literate, articulate and observant, he was chronicler as well as warrior, and those of us who cherish the words of the Civil War soldiers are the beneficiaries of his service to history as well as to our country.

I first encountered Bogardus' letters to the *Poughkeepsie Daily Eagle* some fifteen years ago as I pursued my research on the 5th New York Volunteer Infantry, Duryée's Zouaves. He was among several score of volunteers who left their homes in the Hudson Valley to join that proud and colorful regiment, which was preparing to depart Manhattan for the battlefields of Virginia. The "Old Fifth" included a greater than average number of educated professionals, clerks, lawyers, college students and businessmen— among its enlisted personnel, but Bogardus stood out as one who consistently made an effort to record his wartime experiences and share them with his hometown community.

The full extent of Stephen Bogardus' correspondence eluded me during my brief research trip to Poughkeepsie, and it thus came as a welcome surprise when Joel Craig, himself a descendant of a Duryée Zouave, ferreted out the dozens of missives that comprise this record of wartime experience.

Thanks to Joel's diligent efforts a more complete picture has emerged, encompassing not only Bogardus' service in the Zouaves, but his equally fascinating tenure with the Purnell Maryland Legion.

Stephen Bogardus was a patriotic man of staunch Republican principles. Like most Federal soldiers his sense of duty was inspired by a heartfelt belief in the sanctity of the Union, a loyalty born of devotion to the nation and the sacrifices of its founding fathers. For Bogardus patriotism was not "a mere word," and like soldiers before and since, he justifiably scorned those who were physically able, but unwilling to assume the obligation of defending their country on the field of battle. He had little use for stay at home patriots, and even less for those whose loyalty was questionable, the "traitors at home" as he put it. Moreover, Bogardus viewed the secession of the Southern states as inviting European intervention, all the more reason, he believed, to "Show an undivided front to the enemies of our country."

While not an abolitionist in a humanistic or libertarian sense, Bogardus was nonetheless an outspoken opponent of the "Peculiar Institution." From first hand knowledge gained on campaign in the South, he came to view slavery as degrading to the moral and industrial potential of the regions where it existed. An industrious Yankee to the core, Bogardus saw slavery and the secessionists who supported it as fostering indolence, apathy and economic decline on the part of the white population, rendering "wretched and squalid" those who were inherently capable of greater efforts and accomplishments. For Bogardus the destruction of slavery became a vital and a necessary adjunct to the defeat of the Southern Confederacy.

Stephen Bogardus was capable, competent and brave. He was a loyal subordinate and a good soldier, whose promotion came as well-merited recognition of his abilities. He cherished a heartfelt affinity for the comradeship of service, a nobility of spirit that persisted, even flourished, amidst the hardships and ever-present threat of death, and he personally bore the scars of wounds received in battle. While not blind to incompetence and military mismanagement, his letters do not dwell upon the negative or indulge in tedious grumbling. Ambitious to succeed in the profession of arms, dedicated to his country and cause, zealously idealistic in his sense of nationhood—Stephen Bogardus exemplified the worthiest and best attributes of the Federal soldier. This volume is a tribute not only to one articulate patriot and the regiments in which he served, but to all those who cheerfully took upon themselves the sacred obligation of preserving the United States.

Brian C. Pohanka
Alexandria, Virginia

Introduction

"Were I an author, what a romance could I weave; But I am no writer—nothing but a soldier fighting for his country's honor."

Stephen H. Bogardus, Jr. February 10, 1862

On Saturday, April 13, 1861, the telegraph wires lining the banks of the majestic Hudson River carried news of war to the riverside community of Poughkeepsie, New York. Editor Isaac Platt immediately set his compositors to work on a special edition of the *Poughkeepsie Daily Eagle*. The headlines of the *Eagle* proclaimed the news that Fort Sumter in Charleston Harbor, South Carolina, had been fired on by forces of the newly formed Confederate States of America. The long-feared hostilities that would plunge the nation into bloody civil war had begun. Certainly Isaac Platt and the citizens of Poughkeepsie could not have predicted what the next four years would bring.

Platt quickly took the lead in preparing his community for the coming war. His familiarity with Poughkeepsie's prominent citizens and his ability to speak to the populace through his newspaper made him a natural rallying point in this time of crisis. The owner/editor of the *Eagle* had been publishing newspapers since he was 21 years old; now in his late fifties, Platt had wielded his editorial powers unmercifully against his political enemies for decades. His fiery editorials reinforced his newspaper's motto, which bluntly proclaimed that the *Eagle* was "Neutral in Nothing."

Platt made a personal appeal to the young men of Poughkeepsie to come to the aid of their country in this time of peril. He was well acquainted with many of them, serving as a political mentor to those who seemed destined to be leaders in business or politics. One such acquaintance was 22-year-old Stephen H. Bogardus, Jr., a handsome, congenial and charismatic youth who was employed as a clerk in his father's harness shop on Main St. Bogardus had impressed Platt as an intelligent and articulate young man destined for prominence in Poughkeepsie politics.

Stephen Bogardus was born on June 6, 1838 to Stephen H. Bogardus and Sophia Ann Trevett. He was a descendant of the distinguished Everardus Bogardus, the first Dutch Reformed minister to settle in New York. His family tree included many prominent religious, political and military leaders. His great grandfather was a Revolutionary War veteran and his great uncle was General Robert Bogardus who had served in the War of 1812. Bogardus' father had instilled his son at an early age with the principles that hard work and sound business practices could cure any societal ills. The elder Bogardus believed that any region without a well-developed industrial base was a reflection of the laziness or incompetence of the citizenry. These ideas greatly influenced his son's political views, particularly in regards to that "peculiar institution" known as slavery.

Young Bogardus often accompanied his father on business trips or to visit relatives and as a result became familiar with many of the people and places in the region. As a student he was proficient in writing and mathematical skills, traits which he learned to balance with his natural desires for camaraderie and adventure. By the spring of 1861 he had begun to grow weary of his position as bookkeeper and heir apparent to his father's business. Harness making and leatherwork were not the future to which he aspired. His interest in politics and curiosity about the world beyond the Hudson Valley had reached their peak when news of war arrived that April. Like so many other young men of his generation, Stephen Bogardus would grow to manhood in the camps and on the battlefields of America's Civil War.

On April 18, the *Eagle* announced that a meeting would be held to form a military company of local volunteers. That evening City Hall was packed as prominent businessmen, politicians and militia officers addressed the enthusiastic crowd. As the rally came to a close the eager patriots were called to come forward and volunteer their services in defense of their country. Forty-nine men signed the resolution, which read "We hereby form ourselves into a volunteer Company of Infantry, to be offered to the Governor of this state for immediate service." Conspicuously near the top of the list was the signature of Stephen H. Bogardus, Jr., one of the first Poughkeepsians to volunteer for the War.

As days went by a patriotic frenzy gripped the city as homes, shops and public buildings were decked with flags and bunting, bands played patriotic tunes on the street corners, politicians denounced the southern traitors and every young man vowed to go and fight the rebels. It quickly became apparent, however, that a company of volunteers from Poughkeepsie would be a long time coming. While plenty of Poughkeepsians were willing to shoulder a musket, it seemed none had the organizational skills, coupled with the political connections, to prepare these men for active service. The *Eagle* impatiently railed against the local militia companies who attended patriotic functions and paraded through the streets, but somehow never managed to join the throngs of recruits headed towards the seat of war. Many of Poughkeepsie's patriots began to look elsewhere for an opportunity to enlist.

On the evening of April 22, Stephen Bogardus and childhood friend Alfred Atkins boarded a train for New York City, determined to enlist in one of the regiments forming there. Edmund Platt, Isaac's nephew, recorded that there were "several thousand people at the depot to see them off, they fired cannons and cheered tremendously." Upon their arrival in New York City, Bogardus and Atkins enlisted in a regiment being recruited as the "Advance Guard" or "Duryée's Zouaves". The regiment was to be commanded by Col. Abram Duryée, a wealthy Manhattan businessman with decades of experience as a militia officer. Duryée had wisely chosen West Point graduates and men with prior militia experience to serve as his officers. Among these was former West Point instructor and army engineer Gouverneur K. Warren who would serve as the regiment's Lieutenant Colonel. The regiment promised to be one of the best in the field and the colorful French Zouave uniforms only served to enhance that reputation. The decision of Bogardus and Atkins to enlist in Duryée's Zouaves influenced many of their acquaintances to do likewise.

The regiment received rudimentary military instruction at Fort Schuyler on the East River where they spent several weeks learning to march and drill. Bogardus and Atkins were assigned to Company C in which Bogardus was appointed 2nd Corporal. The "Poughkeepsie Boys" strove to become model soldiers while at the same time adjusting to their urban comrades and surroundings. In May, Isaac Platt visited Fort Schuyler and found Bogardus and the others "arrayed in the wild, picturesque, Saracenic costume of the Zouaves." He reported that they were "in fine, vigorous, hopeful condition, almost spoiling for a fight." While friends and family at home were concerned that army life and immoral comrades might corrupt the impressionable young men, Platt reassured them that they "are earnest Christians, and their influence is already felt among their comrades. We believe they will be valiant soldiers; and disgrace neither themselves, nor their homes, nor their God."

On May 23 the Zouaves paraded through the streets of Manhattan to Broadway where Alfred Atkins recorded that the regiment performed "several maneuvers for the edification of the admiring thousands." After a ceremony and inspection by the mayor the regiment embarked on the voyage to Fortress Monroe near the confluence of the York and James Rivers. Here Bogardus and his comrades set foot on enemy soil for the first time. The regiment had barely gotten settled near the fort at Camp Hamilton, when they received their first call to action. On June 10 Duryée's Zouaves participated in the disastrous Battle of Big Bethel, the first real land engagement of the war. Although the contest went badly for the Union, Duryée's Zouaves received widespread acclaim for their actions.

In July the regiment was ordered to Baltimore, Maryland to perform garrison duty in a city prone to violence and smoldering with undisguised southern sympathies. The Zouaves quickly set about fortifying Federal Hill, an eminence that towered above the city and provided a vantage point from which artillery could control all avenues of approach. While the men were initially disappointed at leaving the theater of active operations, they soon found Baltimore's social life to be a pleasant diversion from their soldierly duties.

It was from Baltimore that Bogardus addressed his first letter to the *Eagle*. Dated October 8, Bogardus began his missive by hoping that "a letter from me would be acceptable." The letter was certainly deemed acceptable as Bogardus proved to be an articulate writer as well as a keen observer. He continued to describe his experiences to the *Eagle* throughout the war, frequently mentioning the landscapes and physical surroundings of the places through which he passed. His vignettes of those whom he encountered brought his writings to life and portrayed the human drama of individuals caught up in the conflict. Whether describing the "compressed lip with its occasional twitching" of Union General Franz Sigel or the convivial hospitality of a corpulent hostess, Bogardus introduced these characters to his readers as he brought them along on his wartime adventures. Throughout his correspondence he boldly stated his Republican political views and his confidence in ultimate victory for the Union. This endeared him to Editor Platt who often had to contend with a restless and war-weary populace at home. As the war dragged on the letters became shorter and less frequent. The demands of military life left little time for lengthy narratives to the folks back home.

On October 19, Bogardus received a promotion to Sergeant. In a regiment populated with exceptional young men, Bogardus was recognized as one who excelled in his duties and possessed the qualities of intelligence and leadership. While most men would have been content to receive the advance in rank, Bogardus had come to realize that he held the necessary qualities to accept even larger responsibilities. Like many of his comrades Bogardus was looking for an officer's commission. He got his chance in November when six companies of Duryée's Zouaves were detailed to accompany an expedition along the Maryland-Virginia shore. Among the troops participating in the operation was a regiment of loyal Marylanders designated as Purnell's Legion. Bogardus struck up a friendship with some of the officers whom he described as "a fine set of fellows, very sociable indeed." He quickly managed to parlay this friendship into a commission and on November 20, Lieutenant Colonel I. G. Johannes wrote to Colonel G. K. Warren requesting Bogardus' transfer to his regiment. Johanness stated that "the service of such men as Sergeant Bogardus is very much desired (he being highly recommended) to assist me in my endeavors to discipline my very green regiment." On December 10, Bogardus became 2nd Lieutenant of Company H, Purnell's Maryland Legion.

Bogardus' clerical abilities soon proved to be an asset to his new regiment and he was appointed Regimental Adjutant, which placed him in charge of the flood of military paperwork. This position excused him from many mundane duties and provided plenty of opportunity to travel about the countryside on official business. Bogardus managed to endear himself to his superiors as well as satisfy his curious and adventurous nature.

Purnell's Legion spent the spring of 1862 chasing "Stonewall" Jackson's Confederate army up and down Virginia's Shenandoah Valley. Bogardus realized the strategic importance of the Shenandoah when he contended that "The Confederate troops with the immense supplies cut off that are in this valley, will be as children in the hands of the Federals." However Jackson proved equal to the challenge, baffling his opponents and defeating them piecemeal, the Confederate general managed to clear much of the Valley of Union forces before joining Lee in the campaign near Richmond. In August Purnell's Legion joined General John Pope's army as it campaigned against Lee and Jackson in northern Virginia. The campaign ended in an embarrassing Union defeat at the Battle of Second Bull Run.

The defeat at Second Bull Run allowed General Robert E. Lee's Army of Northern Virginia to cross the Potomac and advance into Maryland. The stage was set for the bloody confrontation near Sharpsburg, Maryland known as the Battle of Antietam. The battle began just before dawn on September 17 when General Joseph Hooker's I Corps passed through a large cornfield and attacked the Confederate left flank. In support of Hooker's I Corps was General Joseph K. Mansfield's XII Corps, which included Purnell's Legion. Bogardus described the ghastly scene in the cornfield as "a horrible sight," the dead "lying in all positions. Here, one shot through the heart; there, one with his leg torn off; and still farther on, a trunk without a head."

The fighting surged back and forth throughout the morning. Towards noon the Legion was ordered into a forested area known as the West Woods. The movement left them in a vulnerable position in which they came under heavy fire from a regiment of North Carolinians. Scores of brave Marylanders were cut down in the hail of bullets. Near the edge of the woods Adjutant Bogardus, mounted on his horse, presented an inviting target as he worked to steady the wavering line. A Confederate ball soon found its mark, smashing into Bogardus' jaw, knocking out teeth and tearing off part of his upper lip, the impact knocking him from the saddle. On the bloodiest day in American history Stephen H. Bogardus, Jr., shed some of that blood.

Fortunately for Bogardus his wound, though painful and disfiguring, proved to be relatively minor. He was taken to a field hospital near Keedysville, Maryland where he recovered enough to travel home to Poughkeepsie for further recuperation. Eventually he grew a large, drooping mustache to help conceal the scars left by the wound. In December he received a promotion to 1st Lieutenant.

The year 1863 was mostly uneventful for Bogardus and Purnell's Legion. The regiment spent its time doing garrison duty near Frederick, Maryland, guarding Confederate prisoners at Fort Delaware and chasing marauding bands of Confederate cavalry along the Maryland-Virginia border. But the spring of 1864 saw Purnell's Legion called to action once more. General Ulysses S. Grant's bloody spring offensive had decimated the Union army in the battles of the Wilderness and Spotsylvania. In order to carry on his relentless campaign against Lee's army and the Confederate capital at Richmond, Grant needed fresh troops. Purnell's Legion was among those called from garrison duty to the front lines. The Legion was assigned to the Army of the Potomac's V Corps, led by Bogardus' old regimental commander, General Gouverneur K. Warren.

Purnell's Legion participated in the bloody fighting near Cold Harbor, Virginia at the beginning of June, losing several dozen men during the constant skirmishing and artillery bombardments. Bogardus noted, "There is heavy firing day and night somewhere in the army." By mid-June Grant had pinned down Lee's army near the strategic railroad center of Petersburg, Virginia. The resulting siege lasted for months as Grant tried to cut the few remaining rail links leading to Richmond. One of these attempts occurred in mid-August as Warren's V Corps moved against the Weldon Railroad.

In the resulting battle Bogardus was wounded once again as a Confederate shell exploded nearby, killing his horse and knocking him momentarily unconscious. Though barely able to stand, Bogardus took charge of the regiment and manned the breastworks with his men until being relieved by one of his subordinates. Bogardus staggered to a nearby outbuilding where he lay in great pain for several hours. Upon hearing that only five officers were left with the regiment, Bogardus returned to the front lines where he helped organize the battle-weary unit and supervised the distribution of rations. Though still suffering from shock and in constant pain, Bogardus remained on the front lines throughout the night with nothing but a wool blanket to shelter him from the pouring rain. The following day Purnell's Legion was ordered to the rear and Bogardus, with the assistance of several enlisted men, accompanied the regiment on foot, as he was unable to mount a horse. By the following day the pain had become so intense that he reported to the regimental hospital. Bogardus remained at the hospital for two days until orders arrived for the Legion to return to the front. Bogardus, not wanting his men to consider him a "shirk or a coward," rejoined his regiment on the march. His legs and feet were so swollen that he was unable to put on his boots, and, after being hoisted upon a horse, he rode towards the battlefield in his stocking feet. The regiment proceeded to Reams Station where they manned a line of breastworks in anticipation of an attack. Bogardus must have presented a strange sight as he moved among the men, still in his stocking feet and holding his sword in his hand due to the inability to buckle his sword belt around his waist. After several hours it became apparent that the Confederates would not renew the attack and Bogardus returned to the regimental hospital where the surgeon placed him in an ambulance and ordered him to report to the division hospital. From there he was transferred to a hospital in Washington, D.C. where he was still recovering from his wounds when Purnell's Legion mustered out of service in October. On October 22, the *Eagle* heralded the homecoming of the twice-wounded hero and noted, "He is full of confidence in the speedy triumph of the armies of the Union." Bogardus had returned to Poughkeepsie at an opportune time and proved to be a welcome addition to Isaac Platt's political arsenal. The presidential campaign had reached a fever pitch in Poughkeepsie and a bona fide war hero just returned from the front was exactly what Platt needed. Bogardus, along with many of Poughkeepsie's returned veterans, marched in the parades, attended Union rallies, and voted overwhelmingly for Lincoln and the continuation of the war.

    Bogardus did not rest on his laurels for long. Shortly after Lincoln's landslide reelection he began recruiting a company in anticipation of returning to the front. Despite a shortage of willing, able-bodied young men, Bogardus managed to raise a company within a few months. His promise that "promotions will be made from the ranks and for merit alone," combined with his charismatic, friendly nature undoubtedly encouraged men to enlist under his command. By the end of January his company was ready, but it would not be until March 28, 1865 that Captain Bogardus and his men would officially be mustered in as Company E, 192nd New York State Volunteers. The regiment reported to the Shenandoah Valley just in time to witness the ending of hostilities. With General Lee's surrender on April 9, peace returned to the battle-scarred state of Virginia. Company E continued to serve on occupation duty throughout the spring and summer before being mustered out on August 28, 1865. By that time Bogardus had received a brevet promotion to the rank of Major for "faithful and meritorious service."

    The war was over and millions of men returned home. But for Stephen Bogardus there was no going back. He had found a home in the military, had found the adventure he sought, had grown to be a leader of men and had seen his beloved country reunited. He was no longer Stephen Jr., a clerk in his father's store; he was an officer in the United States Army, a veteran of many a bloody battlefield, and a man whose leadership qualities could not be wasted running a small family business. Despite the pain of his war wounds Bogardus decided to make a career in the army. On May 4, 1866 he received a commission as 2nd Lieutenant in the 4th U.S. Infantry.

    But the peacetime regular army was a far cry from the armed host that had fought and marched for four bloody years. Post-war downsizing left few vacancies in the officer corps and those that did occur were likely to be at remote outposts in the far west. Bogardus was initially assigned to Plattsburg Barracks near the Canadian border until December of 1866. The following year found him stationed in Nebraska and the Dakota Territory. He remained in Dakota until August of 1869 when his regiment was transferred to Wyoming. On January 17, 1871, during yet another military downsizing, Bogardus was relieved from active duty and given an honorable discharge; the army no longer had need of his services.

While in active service Bogardus had repeatedly sought treatment by army doctors for relief from the effects of his war wounds. Upon his discharge from the army he found work as a clerk for a railroad company. Throughout the 1870's Bogardus led a nomadic life, following the railroad through Missouri, Arkansas, Texas and finally New Mexico. He continued to suffer from the effects of his wounds and by the age of 42, in 1880, was "totally unfit to perform manual labor of any kind." He was often confined to his bed and suffered from "severe pain in the legs and feet, causing him to walk with the greatest difficulty" as well as "weakness in the back, kidneys and loins" and had only limited use of his right hand. His disabilities eventually made it impossible for him to perform his clerical duties.

By 1892 his physical and financial condition had deteriorated to the point that he was "a permanent cripple" who was "too poor to pay the expense of a visit from a doctor." Bogardus had to resort to using "such simple remedies as he can procure through charity and from humane persons." Stephen H. Bogardus, Jr. had paid a very high personal price to ensure that the country he loved would remain united. He answered the Last Roll on New Year's Day, 1907 and was buried with military honors at Santa Fe National Cemetery, New Mexico.

Dear Eagle

Poughkeepsie Daily Eagle

[NEUTRAL IN NOTHING.]

April 26, 1861

POUGHKEEPSIE BOYS OFF FOR WAR

Messrs. Alfred Atkins, Stephen H. Bogardus Jr., Daniel Brinckerhoff, and James Van Wagner, have joined Col. Duryea's Regiment of Volunteers.

May 20, 1861

OUR BOYS AT FORT SCHUYLER

Poughkeepsie may well be proud of her representatives in Col. Duryea's Regiment. Having an opportunity presented the other day while in the city, we made an excursion to the Fort, where for several weeks this Regiment has been quartered. There are some twenty Poughkeepsie boys enrolled upon its rolls, and we found among them a warm reception. They were arrayed in the wild, picturesque, Saracenic costume of the Zouaves; and for this reason, as well as on account of the "tanning" of their exposed faces, it was somewhat difficult to decipher or recognize them. They are in fine, vigorous, hopeful condition, but almost "spoiling for a fight." Under the system of a "six hours" daily drill, they are in no danger of losing their appetites or of getting the dyspepsia. Several of these young men are earnest Christians, and their influence is already felt among their comrades. We doubt not that they remember Dudley Tyng's thrilling injunction to "stand up for Jesus." We believe they will be valiant soldiers; and disgrace neither themselves, nor their homes, nor their God.

Poughkeepsie Daily Eagle

[NEUTRAL IN NOTHING.]

Camp Federal Hill, Baltimore, Md.
Monday, Oct. 8, 1861

Dear Eagle:
    Supposing as you take an interest in everything pertaining to Po'keepsie thought a letter from me would be acceptable. I think I will tell you what little news is stirring here. In the first place let me tell you that the Poughkeepsie Boys are well thought of in the regiment. The officers make non-commissioned officers of them. Even our old friend Atkins, who, like Caesar's wife, was above suspicion, has been made a corporal. So you see the name of Po'keepsie will not soon fade.
    Supposing your readers would like to hear about our batteries I would say that they are almost finished, and we are mounting the guns daily, and we expect soon to have 64 guns mounted, all of them 42 lbs Columbiads. They will command the whole city of Baltimore and the adjacent territory. Visitors flock by every day to view the works and the Zou Zous as they affectionately call us. A slight difference between them and our friends in Virginia, who nicknamed us "Red Devils". The inhabitants of the "Monument City" treat us very courteously and we are overrun with invitations to dinner and supper, most of which we are compelled to decline. In fact I have now in my possession an invitation to a "Sociable" to be held this evening, and which I am compelled to refuse, although it was arranged especially for me.

The paymaster was here last week, and liquor in abundance is to be found in camp. But this state of affairs will not last, for those that are constantly intoxicated are soon out of money. Even still, it was to the 5th Regiment's credit that among the troops here the 5th exceeds in sobriety and discipline. When the boys were last paid off the Post Office was crowded with our soldiers eager to send home some part of their pay.

We have been battling a new foe, this being a sort of red and yellow clay, streaked with yellow and white sand. We have been kept occupied by working in the trenches. It is strange to see men who never before knew hard labor work away with pick axe or shovel. They carry on as if they had been used to such work all the days of their lives. Their hands — which at home knew nothing heavier than a kid glove, were covered with blisters which they did not mind, but worked until the drum beat the tattoo. All this was done as systematic as if done to Hardee's Tactics. But my paper is getting long and I must close with the promise of writing something in the future. Wishing a long life to the paper and the success of the Republican ticket. I remain yours, & etc.

S.H. Bogardus, Jr.
Comp. C, 5th Reg.

𝔓𝔬𝔲𝔤𝔥𝔨𝔢𝔢𝔭𝔰𝔦𝔢 𝔇𝔞𝔦𝔩𝔶 𝔈𝔞𝔤𝔩𝔢

[NEUTRAL IN NOTHING.]

Camp Federal Hill
Wednesday, Oct. 16, 1861

Dear Eagle:

I saw by a paper that was sent to me that my letter proved acceptable, so here is another. I have just returned from bathing. We have a splendid place for it in the Patapsco River, about half a mile from camp. The Patapsco at that point is about the width of the Hudson at Tappan Zee, but there is no such scenery, no such associations clinging to it now. The works of improvement that we find along the banks of the lordly Hudson, the pride of the North. All is desolation and solitude, except on the summit of the opposite mountains, where in the sunlight gleam the white tents of the Michigan Regiment. We can see the long bridge with its line of sentinels over which that funeral cortege, (where the body proved to be concealed weapons) attempted to cross. The many and vigilant sentinels were too cute for the daughters of the South.

On our way to and from the place of bathing we pass through the yard of the Maryland Blast Works. Where once was activity all now is silence. Where once a hundred men gained a living, naught is seen but the spider as he lazily spins his web over the door-ways and furnace mouths. A little ways and the spectator comes upon another scene of unexampled activity. It is the shipyard where the government alters the steamers into gunboats and transports. What a contract! But I will leave this till another day and inform your readers about ourselves.

We have a great deal more liberty than at Camp Hamilton, and I am sorry to say that some are found mean spirited enough to abuse it. But not many. I suppose we will be moved inside the fortifications in a few days. We are supplied with water from the City Works, and as the pipes are buried far beneath the surface of the earth, no such casualty as befell the gallant Mulligan can overtake us. Last Saturday Company I, Capt. Joseph E. Hamblin, went on an excursion to Westminister for the purpose of seizing some arms that were concealed in a schoolhouse. They were also in strong hopes of capturing the owners of the property. Unfortunately they did not succeed in the latter, but the arms and accoutrements they brought back with them. They frightened the "Secesh" to whom the stuff belonged by the mere sound of their name. In fact we can disperse any crowd of disputants in the city by having some one start the cry of "the Zouaves are coming." Company I returned from their expedition Sunday, followed by a crowd of spectators. They were received with cheers.

Perhaps you would like to hear how we amuse ourselves. As the evenings begin to lengthen, we have to devise some means to help us pass away our spare time. Among a hundred men however this is not very hard work. We have singing, dancing and music at our company streets. The other evening, in company with some mischievous persons, I amused myself by pinning the boys in couples fast to their own tents. After this was "played out" I saw some of the boys bring out a blanket. What was to come next we wondered. But we were not left long in doubt, for having secured a victim, they proceeded to toss him up in the aforesaid blanket, in a style that would have done credit to any lodge of the Sons of Malta. Fortunately our uniform having so much superfluous dry-goods, permits us to do this with impunity. But still it is a species of amusement similar to that in the fable of the "boys and the frogs."

We occasionally have a concert, in which the performers consist of the best that can be picked out in the Regiment; consequently they are much applauded and draw good audiences. Most of the officers attend and occasionally they bring some of their numerous lady friends. Last night we had another, which is considered superior to any that preceded it. Poughkeepsie was not left unrepresented, for among the performers was Mr. Jos. Tyndell. All the pieces were encored, and some of them had to be repeated. This is a kind of amusement that affords pleasure without pain, like the cup that cheers and not inebriates.

I am informed that Mr. Atkins did not like the use I made of his name, so you can make for me a public apology. I did not intend to hurt his feelings, but simply to let his friends know that he was in the way of a promotion.

I was sorry to see by the papers that two such strong Republicans as Fanning and A.B. Smith, were heading a hybrid ticket composed, with this exception, of worn out Democratic politicians. Perhaps though I may be thought digressing from my course, but I am and I hope always will be in favor of Republican principles. Accept my best wishes. I remain yours, & etc. S.H.B. Jr.

Poughkeepsie Daily Eagle

[NEUTRAL IN NOTHING.]

Camp Federal Hill, Baltimore, Md.
Sunday, Oct. 27th, 1861

Dear Eagle:

    On this fine Sabbath morning I will try and write another letter for the edification of your numerous readers. We are now inside the fortifications, having finished them last week. As we have no room inside the works for drill we use an elevated plain about half a mile from here. This place is in the neighborhood of a battery that was erected in 1812 by the Americans for the purpose of resisting the British fleet, which attempted to capture the city of Baltimore. It effected its object, for the British were not aware of its existence. The Admiral of the fleet (whose name I forget), having passed the Fort, sent up signals to notify his Commander that the city would soon be his, when the guns of the battery opened on him, sinking several vessels of the fleet.

    What a change has taken place since that time. Then fortifications were erected to repel invasion from foreign enemies;— now for the purpose of awing traitors at home. I visited the place once some time ago out of motives of curiosity, but as I approached a feeling of awe took possession of me and I reverently uncovered my head. It was indeed consecrated ground, and I thought if those who had shed their blood in defense of their country's flag were looking down upon us they would bless us.

But this will be considered digression. You will pardon me, however I know.

We drill in the afternoon with knapsacks as per Gen. McClellan's order. Although it was at first irksome, yet now that we are used to it we do not mind it in the least. In this drill which consists of the battalion, we execute several maneuvers that are new to most regiments and will not interest any of your readers except those who understand military tactics. Suffice it to say that "double quick" is one of them.

A new flag staff has been erected on a prominent part of the hill and from the top of it floats a handsome flag, presented by the citizens of Baltimore. Perhaps I should have said the ladies of the "Monumental City," for they are the donors. In fact the ladies of the city are the most enthusiastic in the cause for which we are fighting. We have hundreds of them to witness our evening parade. We are obliged to have it in Warren street, owing to the scarcity of space on the hill.

We have made on Federal Hill a fort that in two or three years will compare favorably with those in the neighborhood of the "Empire City". I mean in beauty and style. It is considered one of the lions of Baltimore. Are you going up to Federal Hill to see the "Zouaves" is a very common question among the inhabitants. Col. Warren, who has been very sick, has almost entirely recovered and will soon resume command. I don't know how my old acquaintances would like to sleep with no other shelter than is afforded by a tent, while the post was lying on the ground; but when I say I have gained nine pounds they can see how I stand it. In fact the members of the regiment are healthier than when at home. So you can see that although we miss the pleasures of home, yet we gain in health.

I have just returned from the depot, where the 20th Regiment has just stopped. I saw our old friends, Capt. Smith and others, all of whom wish to be remembered to their friends

in Poughkeepsie. They were in good health and spirits, but slightly fatigued with their journey. I hope and trust that they will do good service, and that Dr. Tuthill will not have too many limbs to amputate. Before this reaches you they will have reached their destination. God speed them and grant them a safe return from the war. But I have written all the news, so I had better stop.
Goodbye.
S.H.B., Jr.

Poughkeepsie Daily Eagle

[NEUTRAL IN NOTHING.]

Camp Federal Hill, Baltimore, Md.
Sunday, Nov. 10, 1861

Messrs. Editors:

Allow me first to congratulate you on the glorious victory secured by your efforts. I mean at the late election. This state also gave an overwhelming majority in favor of the Union as it is, and the enforcement of the laws. There were fewer disturbances than common. I believe there were only two or three persons killed; something unparalleled in the annals of Baltimore for late years. Of course there were a great many arrests of persons charged with secession proclivities, but thanks to Gen. Dix's proclamation;— these were fewer than we expected.

Co. A. of this Regiment were sent the day before to Westminister to guard the polls, as some trouble was expected. The secession ticket of course was styled the National Democratic ticket. We have now a picket station for this regiment at Locust Point. The steamer Belvedere, one of the Great Expedition, lies near the wharf half wrecked; and as the neighborhood is not as steadfast to the Union as we should like it, we have a guard there. Night before last the regiment slept on their arms, expecting an attack on the steamer. But we were not disturbed, although we were all willing to hear once more the long roll, a sound which has not fallen on our ears for some time.

The rumor throughout the Camp is that we are to be stationed here for the winter. How true this report is I do not know, but in confirmation of it, next week will witness the commencement of barracks. In fact we are now kept very close, only two of each company are allowed to go to the city each day. Visitors, however, are allowed inside the fortifications as usual. And their number is not small, for every man in the regiment has friends in the city who make it a point to call on him as often as possible.

Last night for the first time we built fires in the company streets, and as they blazed up it seemed as though the hill was on fire. It was a magnificent sight to stand away from the fire to see the fiery stream through the branches of the trees, while the dark forms of the men as they seemed to flit to and fro around the blaze, appeared like spectres. It was indeed a picture for an artist.

I can hardly find any news to fill my sheet. Everything is quiet, although everybody is on the tiptoe of expectation in regard to news from the expedition. The little we have heard has only whetted our appetites, and we await with anxiety further advices. I hear that we have again lost our Colonel, he having been promoted Brigadier General of Volunteers. We have also lost several other officers, and privates are leaving every day for Commissions. Your humble contributor is not one of the favored.

The weather is cold with white frost every morning, yet we don't mind it much. In fact, we have fewer sick persons in the hospital than in extreme warm weather. Of course the knapsack drill is responsible for the large number of the sick who are otherwise well. But my paper is most used up and I must close. S.H.B., Jr.

Poughkeepsie Daily Eagle

[NEUTRAL IN NOTHING.]

In Camp, Near Newtown, Md.
November 16, 1861

Dear Eagle:

    Thinking your readers would be interested in the details of our expedition, I have compiled from my diary that I am keeping, a short sketch for their benefit. On Monday afternoon an order was given to six companies of our regiment to get ready in heavy marching order to leave in the morning. Although the time of our departure was set at seven o'clock A.M., the detachment did not leave Federal Hill until one o'clock P.M. I was detailed with the baggage wagons. I did not accompany the detachment through the city. However it did not reach the boat until three o'clock. The boat did not leave the wharf until four o'clock.

    The name of the boat upon which we embarked was the Pocahontas, and from her appearance I should judge it was almost as old as the original of the cognomen. We were accompanied by the Star, on board of which was the 21st Indiana Volunteers. Quite a number of the citizens of Baltimore were at the wharf to bid us God speed. As we passed Federal Hill we beheld the remainder of the regiment upon the ramparts ready to salute us, cheer upon cheer rang in the air from our party, which was answered by those left behind. As we glided by one of the forty two pounders belched forth it's adieu, and the band struck up the Star Spangled Banner.

Nothing occurred that is different from other voyages of similar nature and night drew around us her sable curtain. Sleep however did not visit many eyes on board, for a more uproarious crowd than Zouaves has never been seen. Morning dawned upon us clear and beautiful. About 11 o'clock A.M. a stream of sand flew up before the bow and a concussion announced that the Pocahontas was aground. At first this only afforded amusement for those on board, but when it was discovered that the efforts of our consort to pull us off the bar, upon which we had stuck, were unavailing, gloom settled down upon us.

To add to our alarm a gunboat was seen in the distance which was soon followed by two others. As their nationality could not be told from the distance, we supposed them to be rebel vessels. We were in a nice predicament. Aground in the Pocomoke Sound far from land, without guns on board, and three of the enemies' vessels bearing down upon us, was enough to make the bravest man among us look blue. You can imagine the change in one's feelings when a boat put off the nearest point with the Stars and Stripes floating from her bow. The fleet proved to be the U.S. gunboat Hercules and two consorts, the names of which I could not learn. They could render no assistance until the tide was at its height which would be almost midnight. A fine prospect was ahead of us indeed. To spend another night aboard that old craft, without any water, it did not make any of us feel pleasant. But I will pass over that night of horror, with the wish that I may never be caught in another one of like nature.

We got afloat about six o'clock on Thursday morning and went about a mile further, where we had to stop again and wait for the Star which was to take us to our destination. After waiting about an hour she hove in sight and was moored alongside. Many a groan rent the air as we left the Pocahontas, and wishes that she might sink before we returned were prevalent.

We soon arrived in the Pocomoke River, glad to see land both sides of us once more.

I have found everything in the Old Dominion built on a crooked scale. I think the pattern must be the Pocomoke River. It is a stream about the width of the Fallkill at the foot of Smith street, but a crookeder river does not exist. It is the perfection of crookedness. Why the distance by water from the mouth of the river to this place is 40 miles, while by land it is only 15 miles. The banks of the river, if banks they can be called, are very flat, reminding me of the flats of New Jersey. Generally they are heavily wooded, although salt marshes were to be seen at intervals. The water of the river is about the color of beer and slightly brackish.

We reached Newtown at 5 P.M. glad to be at our journey's end. Several regiments were here ahead of us and they kindly bade us welcome. The citizens of this place had thronged the banks to see Duryea's Zouaves, about whom they had heard so much from their friends in the Monumental City. Newtown is a busy little place about the size of Pleasant Valley, but not as much scattered. It embraces within its limits three churches, several school houses, and stores of all kinds. What its population is I do not know. It is a strong Union place and welcomed us gladly. It being far from a market provisions are very cheap. Sweet potatoes are selling from fifty cents a bushel, chickens for thirty-five cents a pair, and other things in proportion.

We are encamped about three quarters of a mile from a landing in a large open lot. Encamped with us are several other regiments and detachments, viz: Sixth Michigan volunteers, 500 men; Twenty first Indiana, 500 men; Fourth Wisconsin, 1000; Purnell's Legion of Maryland, 1,000; First Maryland, 700; Second Delaware, 700; Reading Cavalry, Penn., 100; and Nun's battery of 6 pieces from Massachusetts, numbering 100 men. So you can see that we have quite a formidable force.

I believe the rebels are encamped about ten miles from this place, strongly entrenched. They number about 8,000 men, only a part of which are in uniform. We are obliged to wait here eight days, as the proclamation of Gen. Dix gives them that time to disperse and lay down their arms. We have large numbers of visitors, all strong for the Union and the enforcement of the laws. Several have tendered their services as guides and scouts and have been accepted. Our boys have explored the country for miles around in search of persimmons which grow here in abundance. But I must close. We are all well, but anxiously waiting for orders to move forward.
Yours, &,
S.H.B., Jr.

𝔓𝔬𝔲𝔤𝔥𝔨𝔢𝔢𝔭𝔰𝔦𝔢 𝔇𝔞𝔦𝔩𝔶 𝔈𝔞𝔤𝔩𝔢

[NEUTRAL IN NOTHING.]

In Camp, Near Oakhill, Va.,
Accomac Co.,
Nov. 21, 1861

Dear Eagle:

 Here we are again in the Old Dominion, after a tedious march of 17 miles. We left Newtown Sunday morning about 9 o'clock and marched all day. We arrived here about 5 o'clock, P.M., and instantly pitched our tents. The road, for a wonder, was very good. Generally, however, the ground in this part of the country is very level, a slight rise of the ground being denominated a hill. Stones are almost unknown and all fences are built of pine rails.

 Before we left Newtown a rumor prevailed that the rebels had dispersed, but just as we marched it was contradicted. Which report to believe we did not know, so we trudged along hoping to find a "foeman worthy of our steel." As we progressed evidence of the rebels having been ahead of us were visible. Trees were cut down and laid across the road and bridges were destroyed along the road. About 3 P.M. a battery was seen ahead, placed so as to command the road. The bugle sounded a halt and we began to prepare for a conflict. Soon, however, the command to march was given, and we then knew it was untenanted. We soon reached it, and in a few moments the parapets were covered with the "red devils." As we examined it laughs of derision were heard on every side and wishes that the rebels had remained to be attacked were prevalent. Why, the Zouaves could take it in half an hour, was the exclamation of many. It was a burlesque instead of a battery. Boys of 14 would not have owned it for their work. A blow of the foot would crumble half a yard down. The moat, two foot wide and three feet deep, could be properly called a ditch and extended along the front.

    The battery was built in the shape of a V, with one of the sides facing the road. It was about six feet high, with embrasures for 4 guns. Whether they were ever mounted I do not know, as none were visible. However, in one of the embrasures was a log mounted on a wooden swivel facing the road, and at a distance resembling a cannon. We did not stop very long at the battery as there was nothing worth seeing, but moved on and here we are. I don't think we will stay here very long as the rebels are said to be only a few miles ahead. If all their batteries are like the one we have just passed we will have no trouble taking them. We are encamped in a beautiful place, with wood and water in abundance, and handy.

    A sad accident occurred in the Michigan regiment last evening, by which a life was lost. The particulars of the affair I could not learn. It was through the careless use of firearms, however, while loaded. While I am writing the last rites are being paid to all that is left of one who was as gay and light hearted as any of us. The mournful strains of the fife and drum, playing a dirge, fall sadly upon my ear. Poor fellow, shot by comrades, dying and being buried far from home and friends is hard to think of. Had he been killed in battle it would have been satisfaction to his friends to know that he fell doing his duty, fighting manfully and falling with his back to the field and his feet to the foe. But to be killed by an associate is a pitiful thought for the mother who mourns for her boy laid beneath the sod in a stranger's land, his grave an object of curiosity to the passers by.

But I am moralizing while your readers are waiting for some items of news to interest them. But I have nothing to write. We are out of the world and hear no news. Alas, Virginia! — how you have suffered in the hands of your pitiless masters. Where there were once flourishing farms and plantations, all is desolate. The houses are deserted, gardens overrun with weeds, and nothing is to be seen but a few negroes lying in the sun too lazy to do anything more than stare at us. "The wheel at the cistern is broken" indeed, and the Mother of States will rue the day when she cast all into the muddy waters of secession. I doubt whether she will ever entirely recover from the effects of this war.

I have just returned from a visit to Purnell's Legion, so named from it's Colonel. It is a crack regiment of Maryland. The officers are a fine set of fellows, very sociable indeed. The Lieut. Col. Johannes, who was in command, says the material of which the regiment is composed cannot be excelled, but he thinks they need more service. They are mostly from Maryland, picked up along the Pennsylvania line. They go in strong for the Union, the Constitution and enforcement of the laws. The order has just arrived from Gen. Lockwood, who has charge of the Brigade, for our advancing this afternoon at 3 o'clock. I must get my knapsack packed before that time, so adieu.
S.H.B., Jr.

Poughkeepsie Daily Eagle

[NEUTRAL IN NOTHING.]

In Camp, 9 miles from Drummondtown, Va.
November 22, 1861

Dear Eagle:

We arrived here last night, very tired after two days tramp. On Wednesday we traveled to a small village called Temperanceville, about 8 miles from our old camping ground. Yesterday we marched from there to this place, a distance of 26 miles. Many of the men gave out from fatigue and had to be carried in the baggage wagons. Every member of the brigade had blistered feet or lame ankles. We passed on our march through several small villages, but I could learn the name of only one which was called Modesttown From the only hotel in the place, a large American flag was flying. Of course we saluted it with Zouave enthusiasm.

On our way to this place we passed a deserted house, in front at which was a tall flag staff. On the summit of this was a small Union flag. Where the occupants had gone I know not—but nailed to the pole, flaunting in the breeze and defying secession, waved the stars and stripes. The boys hailed this incident with nine hearty cheers, such as only come from the heart. The inhabitants of this country are either very ignorant of distance or have never traveled; for no two are agreed on the length of the road. I have since learned something that accounts for this, namely, that this is Henry A. Wise's Congressional District, in which he boasted there was never newspaper, schoolhouse nor post office.

Most of the white people between Temperanceville and Modesttown are strong Union men; one of them remarking, "this is the Union neighborhood." In connection with this I will mention a laughable scene that occurred on the way to Temperanceville. We had just emerged from a wood where we saw, about a quarter of a mile ahead, a primitive sawmill, not in motion, although a man was in charge. As soon as he spied us he started the wheel and worked as though his life depended on his exertions. At first we saw nothing singular in this, but as we passed a turn in the road we saw a large tree felled across the road. Upon examining the road we found that it was obstructed in a similar manner for two miles in advance. The owner of the sawmill knew nothing about it and could not show us any way to get past them. A pistol presented at his head by one of our officers soon changed his mind and he volunteered to show us another road. He stopped his mill and mounted the Colonel's horse and set off.

While he was gone the boys started the mill and could not stop it. It kept sawing until the log was sawn through. As it could not be stopped it tried to cut the iron— but here a match for it was found, for the teeth of the saw flew fast. What the owner of the mill said I do not know, for just then the bugle sounded Forward, and off we went. We followed the road he pointed out, and had no more trouble. After passing Modesttown we found the secession sentiment predominating, till we reached Drummondtown, where a Union man is a rarity. In fact we found only one Union man in the place, and he was in jail. We passed, before reaching Drummondtown, another battery of 14 guns. The embrasures, however, were so close that if a gun had been fired by the rebels it would have destroyed half of the fortification. The whole concern was no better than the other of which I spoke in a former letter.

Drummondtown, which is the county seat of Accomac, and the headquarters of secession in the peninsula, is an old town dating far back in the past. I believe it was occupied by the British in the war of 1812. In front of the principal hotel was an old cannon that had been captured from the British during the war, planted muzzle first, to serve as a tie post. The place in good times must have been quite a thriving little town, judging from the number of closed doors. A little paint would help the appearance of the houses a great deal. Some of them look as ancient as the cities of the old world.

No business seems to be doing — a sure sign that no Union feeling is allowed to show itself. Find me a place where business is thriving and I can tell you at once that Union sentiment prevails. But show me a town where the stores are closed and the houses deserted, there you will soon see that the place is a hot bed of treason. Thus it is in Drummondtown. It wears a half dead look. The faces of the inhabitants left in Drummondtown were very long as we passed through. We halted on the outskirts for a few minutes only and then marched on. We stayed here long enough, however, to find in the jail a large lot of concealed weapons, accoutrements, & c., including seven pieces of artillery, elegantly mounted. Had we been allowed to search the houses, without doubt we would have discovered enough to supply a regiment. But we had no authority and so refrained from doing it. After we passed this place we marched on as well as our weary condition would allow.

Several incidents occurred to set us in good humor, one of which I must mention. As we passed by a wood a negro appeared who was very much excited at the sight of us. He shouted "Hurrah for the Union," and ended with a whoop that might have been heard for a mile. At the same time he would jump up and down, contorting his body into all kinds of shapes. He made such a laughable sight that every body roared. But I must close

for we are getting ready for another march. The doctor has prohibited the Colonel from going so far again in a day. The remainder of the Poughkeepsie boys are as well as they can be under the circumstances, and send their respects.
Yours, & c.
S.H.B., Jr.

Poughkeepsie Daily Eagle

[NEUTRAL IN NOTHING.]

In Camp, Near Eastville, Northampton Co.
Dec. 14th, 1861

Dear Eagle:
 We arrived here one week ago about 5 o'clock P.M. We bade farewell to Wilson's Branch about 8 A. M., and started for this place, at which we are now encamped. It did not seem much like the Sabbath, but there is scarcely such a thing in war times. Yet we met many on their way to church. We passed through several small villages on our route. We marched through them to the tune of Yankee Doodle. Strange music for a Sunday. We were told after passing through a place called Bel Haven, that the landlord of the only hotel the place could boast, had, in expectation of our stopping in the place, 200 pies sweetened with strychnine. Happily for our friends at home, we did not stop. As he had no use for his pies after our departure he buried them in the woods. Had we known this affair in time, not one house would have remained standing to tell the passerby where the place once stood. And I think the landlord too, would have tried an experiment with one of nature's productions, viz., hemp. But our commander seems to be afraid of hurting the feelings of the secessionists; so he kept the story quiet till we had arrived here.
 At another place, called Francktown, we passed a cart filled with contraband goods, in charge of some of our men. About a mile before reaching Eastville the flag that we had found at Bird's Nest was put upon a pole, Union down, and the

fortunate finder carried it in this manner flying at our head. Long faces were the order of the day in Eastville as we passed, and one woman was seen crying bitterly. On inquiry we found out that she was the maker of the flag, and only a short time ago presented it to the fugitive Colonel Smith, who formerly resided in this place. I think she did not expect her handiwork would return in such a manner, and so soon. As we passed the hotel it was trailed to the dirt and greeted with three groans by the cavalry who were stationed there.

A strange story is told of the rebel Colonel Smith. It is said that when he heard of our arrival at Temperanceville, he left Drummondtown on horseback instantly. He traveled with such speed that when he arrived at the wharf at Cherrystone, about five miles from here, the hound with which he had started was distanced. Eastville, like the rest of the villages which boast Secession as King, is almost deserted. Most of the principal citizens being secessionists have fled. The war has produced a great alteration in the looks of the place; for I should judge that at one time Eastville could boast a flourishing business. It is the county seat of Northampton, and the last place of importance on the peninsula.

About a quarter of a mile back we passed a field of sugar cane. This being the first I ever saw I secured some seeds, which I shall send home. We are stationed in a woods about a mile from Eastville. We have no guard of consequence around the camp, consequently the boys wander about the country to their heart's content. One of the boys and cousin B. found a young opossum—so all the boys are opossum hunting. As yet they have found no more.

Fowls, oysters and sweet potatoes are very cheap, and our principal eating. Oysters of the largest size are selling for 25 cents a bushel; turkeys 50 cents each; and chickens and ducks are 25 cents each. Sweet potatoes the boys eat from morning till night. The price is from 10 to 15 cents a bushel. However, as we were not paid off before leaving Federal Hill, they cannot buy much. We have plenty of fun in cutting down trees. If Uncle Sam has to pay for all the trees that the Zous Zous have cut down it will amount to a pretty round sum. In every forest in which we have encamped we have left our mark.

Another load of concealed arms has been found since we have been here. They were found in the swamp which is at the foot of the wood. The muskets are poor, and the equipments good. The boys are impatient to get back to Baltimore where they can hear what is going on in the outer world. We are as much out of the way of news as if we were confined in a convent. Last Thursday night Col. Warren invited several of the principal secessionists in the neighborhood to a supper. After the supper came a concert. The liquor operated on our guests so much that when we sung the Star Spangled Banner, and Red, White and Blue, they joined in the chorus. I shall believe hereafter that the best thing for converting rebels is whiskey.

We had a review this morning by Gen. Lockwood witnessed by a large number of spectators. The negroes were highly pleased with some of them coming five miles to witness it. After the review we showed the General some of our drilling - he said it was excellent. I have just heard that we are to start for Baltimore tomorrow; taking the back track as far as Pougateague, a village about 25 miles distant.

Yours,

S.H.B., Jr.

Poughkeepsie Daily Eagle

[NEUTRAL IN NOTHING.]

Camp Federal Hill, Baltimore, Md.
December 18, 1861

Dear Eagle:

Here I am at my old resting place. We arrived here Thursday about 10 A.M. We left Eastville Monday morning and marched about 22 miles. We encamped four miles from Pougateague. A snow storm occurred while there. Tuesday morning was beautiful— the cold, bracing air invigorating body and mind. The idea of "going home," as we call it, acted like magic on our fatigued limbs and made us fresh again. We reached the wharf about 11 o'clock and found the steamer Star waiting for us. However, we did not get off as soon as we expected— for the breezes, which seemed so pleasant and refreshing on the land, blew a perfect gale on the water. The bay was so rough that the captain dare not sail. So we spent a night on board of her.

The next morning (Wednesday) the wind had lulled so much that the captain thought it safe to start — so off we set for Baltimore. The water seemed alive with wild ducks, and the boys amused themselves by shooting them with their muskets. We arrived after dark at the dock off Fort McHenry, where we made fast till morning. We entered the city with colors flying. When we reached the Fort the whole garrison, with Major Hull at their head, issued out of the sally port to greet us. We were soon dismissed— and now, having all our tents erected, consider ourselves at home.

Carpenters are erecting barracks for us— they consist of large buildings, 120 feet long and 25 feet wide; they are two stories high, and well built. How they are arranged inside I do not know, not having seen the plan. I understand they are to be better finished than any other buildings of the style in the Union. Yesterday I saw two friends of mine, Major Haskins and John Buasing, from Westchester county, N.Y. They have been engaged in paying off the troops at Hatteras. They represent a deplorable state of things as existing.

We have now a new system of passes— they are, to go to the city from 4 _ P.M. till 9 _ P.M. Ten of each company are allowed every day, and if one comes in behind time or intoxicated it is deducted from the number of passes granted. I am afraid it will not last long, for some will abuse this privilege until it is stopped. Accept my congratulations on the result of the mayoralty election in the great metropolis, and believe me.
Yours truly,

S.H.B., Jr.

Poughkeepsie Eagle Dec. 19, 1861
Our friend and correspondant, Stephen H. Bogardus, Jr., is now in town, seeing his friends. He was formerly Sergeant in Duryea's Zouaves, but has just been promoted 2d Lieutenancy in Co. H, Col. Purnell's Maryland Legion. His many friends will be glad to hear of his good fortune.

Poughkeepsie Daily Eagle

[NEUTRAL IN NOTHING.]

Camp Hamilton,
Dec. 31, 1861

Dear Eagle:

I presume most of your readers will be surprised to see this letter headed as it is, but I could not refrain from writing one from this, our old camp ground. I arrived in Baltimore safely on Saturday morning, and after breakfast took a walk to Federal Hill to see my old companions in the gallant 5th. Most of them were glad to see me and hear from home. They had just moved into barracks and were comfortably situated.

Of course I could not stop long for there was other business for my attendance. And serious too, it proved, for I lay on a sick bed in the Monumental City until Sunday morning. But I had fallen into good hands and was well taken care of. Well I left Baltimore on Sunday evening in the steamer Georgianna. She is a fine boat but will not compare with our North River floating palaces either in speed or accommodations. However, she was my only means of conveyance, and of course I had no alternative.

We arrived safely at this place yesterday about 7 A.M. and I soon found that the hotel was full, so I was in a nice predicament. The boat for Eastville did not leave Fort Monroe until the next day, and here I was, in a strange place, without a "place to rest my weary head." Happily I recollected that the 20th Regiment (Turner Rifles) was encamped at this place, so I proceeded to throw myself on their tender mercies — and well did they act the Good Samaritan for I have never been better treated in my life. They seemed to vie with each other in rendering me those acts of kindness that are proverbial among people of their nationality. As you are well aware Po'keepsie is represented among them, Lieut. Charles Courtenir is the gentleman to whom I am mostly indebted, and he is well known at home. The rest of the boys from Po'keepsie are all well and send their respects home to their friends.

A week ago Sunday an attack was made upon the pickets of this regiment, the particulars of which affray were published in the papers. This place is altered a little since we left it last summer. What recollections crowd my mind as I gaze upon the spot where Duryea's Zouaves marched so gallantly last May, and think of the changes that took place so soon after on the memorable 10th of June when 8 of their number laid down their lives through the blunder of a Yankee politician, as Gen. Pierce is yet called. Truly his skirts can never be cleared of that blood, and Big Bethel will always be remembered against him.

Quite a little stir was caused here Sunday by the boldness of a rebel steamer that hovers around Sewell's Point. The Express, an old tow boat was going to Newport News with a lighter filled with water in convoy. Neither had any guns on board, and as they passed the Point this saucy little craft boldly put out for them. She fired one gun and then running around the steamer fired the second gun before anything could be done to render assistance. To cap the climax, she succeeded in cutting out the schooner of water and took her around the point. It created considerable stir, and this morning a gun boat went with the Express to guard her while she was engaged in the same business.

There is scarcely anything else new in this neighborhood. The Government is hard at work taking care of her soldiers, and an endless task it seems to be. But I must close for there comes the Steamer Geo. Washington to take me to Eastville. I have a great deal to write but I will have to postpone it till my next letter. For the information of my friends I would say that my address will be hereafter Lieut. S. H. Bogardus, Co. H, Purnell's Legion, Eastville, Northampton Co., Va.

S.H.B., Jr.

Poughkeepsie Daily Eagle

[NEUTRAL IN NOTHING.]

Headquarters, Eastville, Northampton Co., Va.
Jan. 15, 1862.

Dear Eagle:
    Although I have not seen your paper for some time, still perhaps you would like to hear again from me. I am pleasantly situated on a neck of land at the intersection of King's Creek, Cherry Stone Inlet and Chesapeake Bay. We are in the midst of "Secesh", where rebels used to run the blockade. Our work consists of overhauling rebels that come this way, and taking care of ourselves. Although I have headed this letter Eastville, still I have visited that place but once since I have been in this vicinity. This place where I am situated is called Townfields, but our headquarters are at the former place and all communications must be addressed accordingly.
    We have had but one brush with the rebels since I have been here and that did not amount to much. There is a great deal of grain on this place which is in our possession and the enemy wished to destroy it, together with the house which we inhabit, for the purpose of getting rid of us. They did not succeed however, although they attacked front and rear. Not long ago Capt. Fulton of this Legion captured a vessel, on board of which was twenty-four boxes of tobacco consigned to parties in Dixie, also the Southern mail that had run the blockade. However, we did not keep them long, for Gen. Lockwood returned them to their owners. Why he did so I do not know, but think in common

with others that a screw is loose somewhere. This is not the first case of the kind that has occurred lately. Whether Gen. Dix will sanction such proceedings remains to be seen. However, we do not relax our own exertions, for upon Lockwood rests the responsibility of such actions.

Occasionally we discovered a mine of concealed weapons or ammunition. Until Saturday Co. H was the only company at this outpost, but that evening a new company, (K) Capt. Patterson, which had just been recruited, came down from Baltimore to stay with us until further orders. They make very good company for us, as their officers are "good fellows", and with them we can while away the long evenings pleasantly. Our living is pretty good, as wild fowl, fresh eggs and oysters abound in our neighborhood. I could astonish some of the staid young men of Po'keepsie by showing them our table at meal time. Never mind boys, I won't excite your envy by mentioning our bill of fare.

One thing however is missed very, very much — that is good female society, for we have nothing here to take the place of the "fair and frail sex". All the substitute is dark complexioned and a rather brunette order of beauty. But unfortunately they are not well posted on the topics of the day. Neither do they keep up with the style of dress laid down in the Gazette of Fashion as the prevailing order of the day. This is a rainy day, and we scarcely know how to while away time.

We had yesterday a snow storm that lasted all day, but changed to rain during the night, and continues to do the latter still. This is the first snow of the season in this neighborhood. It interferes slightly with my arrangements, as on Saturday, while cruising around the creek on business, I discovered a fair young lady about "sweet sixteen" and thought I would call at the house to-day to find out whether her family was "Secesh" or Union in sentiment, in accordance with our orders from Headquarters. This you see is a very good way to get acquainted with the

neighbors. It is about the only way, for they are a very unsociable set. Last Saturday I visited the rebel batteries on the point opposite. This is the best constructed fortification on the Peninsula. It has however gone to decay since the day that our gunboats threw a few shells into it. We questioned the contrabands whom we found at work cutting wood in the vicinity about the gallant defenders of this breastwork. They stated that the first ball caused the brave soldiers, who were fighting to save their homes from pillage and their wives and daughters from rapine and dishonor, took to their heels and fled ignominiously without returning a shot. This is the way that the brave Southerner seems to do whenever he faces the foe, shows his pluck. But I must close as it is most time for retreat or evening parade, and as I am acting Adjutant of the post I must write out my orders. Hoping that this will reach you while you in are good health. I subscribe myself
Yours from Secessia,
S.H.B., Jr.

P.S. – My address is Lieut. S.H. Bogardus, Co. H, Purnell's Legion, Eastville, Northampton Co., Va.
S.H.B., Jr.

Poughkeepsie Daily Eagle

[NEUTRAL IN NOTHING.]

Camp Bay View, Townfield, Va.
Monday, Feb. 10, 1862

Dear Eagle:

It is some time since I wrote to you last, and perhaps you would like to hear again from your old correspondent. Scarcely anything has occurred lately worth noting. In fact, until the last week, we have heard nothing from the northern world on account of bad weather. Saturday was for a rarity a beautiful day, and we sailed to the island that lies about two miles from us. It was formerly a part of the main land, but the connecting land has been washed away by the sea.

The sea is continually encroaching on the land everywhere in this vicinity. At least half of a mile has been washed away from this farm. At low tide, far out in the sea stand rocky formations that once towered far above Neptune's domain. On this plain is an old windmill, once considered the centre of the farm. Soon that will fall and nothing will be seen of the place where it now stands but a dreary waste of water. This is another "irrepressible conflict," that can be witnessed anywhere on this peninsula. But this is a digression that you must pardon. I will return to our voyage before mentioned.

We arrived there without any trouble. This island is about 15 feet above low water mark. The first article we saw was part of a vessel lying high and dry, half imbedded in the sand. What story could be made out of that piece of timber, scarcely 12 feet long! How long it had lain there I could not tell

— nor whence it came. Perhaps it was a part of the wrecked Arctic — the long looked for Pacific — or the anxiously watched for City of Glasgow. Near it lay a ghastly skull, with its hideous grin. Whether it was another relic of the same wreck I do not know — but it set me thinking. What hopes, what fears, were quenched when the vessel went down with its living freight. Perhaps it was but the wreck of some small coaster, which was never heard of more. Somewhere a wife or mother was looking continually for the return of the wanderer, and turning sadly away from the window with the exclamation, "Will he never come?" Wearied with watching, she died brokenhearted, sorrowing for her long lost son or husband. Were I an author, what a romance could I weave out of that log of wood with its luring companion. But I am no writer — nothing but a soldier fighting for his country's honor.

I saw nothing on this island, with this exception, worth noting. Like the rest of this part of Kanawha, it is sandy — producing nothing but sweet potatoes and corn. Perhaps one word in the above sentence needs explanation, viz., Kanawha. Although the inhabitants of the peninsula do not call it anything else than Virginia, still they recognize the authority of Gov. Pierpont. At an election held under his proclamation all the Union candidates were elected by a large vote. But here is another digression.

Well, we left the island, and shaped our course for the North Point lighthouse which lays about three miles from here. We reached it without accident in a short time. It is and has been deserted ever since the breaking out of this war that distracts our once happy country. The keeper, whose name is Floyd (a relative of the notorious John B.), fled for Dixie after destroying all useful property. His books and papers, that he left in his flight, show that he had profited by the example of his illustrious cousin. It must run in the family, I think.

The place was deserted, and with the exception of a stove that he could not remove, nothing of use could be found. The floor was strewn with the remains of property destroyed. However, he left his government blanks, which are now in our possession. We struck the fog bell several times, and it rang dismally over the deep, startling the gulls from the water—and they circled round the lighthouse with discordant cries. The bell was covered with their excrement, and for many a day had served them for a roosting place. They were angry, no doubt, at us for disturbing the silence of the place. This lighthouse is strongly resting upon fluted columns of solid iron. It is not very high, but contains a great deal of room. There are two tanks of water, still full, and parts of the lamp are in different parts of the building. But they are of no use, for there is no keeper to collect them and have the lamp lit. After looking through the building we started for home, where we arrived safely in time for dinner.
Yours as usual,
S.H.B., Jr.

𝔓𝔬𝔲𝔤𝔥𝔨𝔢𝔢𝔭𝔰𝔦𝔢 𝔇𝔞𝔦𝔩𝔶 𝔈𝔞𝔤𝔩𝔢

[NEUTRAL IN NOTHING.]

Headquarters Co.'s H & K, Camp Bayview, Va.
March 8, 1862

Dear Eagle:
    Cold, blustering March is upon us, with its chill winds freezing the marrow in our bones, and driving back the blood to it's source. This is the most unpleasant month in the year in the South. Instead of seeming the commencement of spring it seems to be the height of winter. But I will leave this description to Thompson who has described it far better than I could. Last Tuesday having received an invitation from my friend Dr. J. G. Potts, whose address I sent you, to visit his new residence, which is the light house on Hog Island, I in company with my friend Lieut. Watkins left Townfields early and commenced our journey.
    By the by, I will digress a little here to relate an anecdote of the doctor. At his former residence in Drummondtown the rebels raised a company of artillery. The news arrived that the federal gunboats were to attack Pangoteague. As there was nobody in either place that understood artillery practice, our friend Potts, who had "been thro' the mill" in the old country, was impressed into the service by the rebels and told to take command of the battery which consisted of one gun. This he did, taking with him as his only assistant an ignorant German. When the order was given to load, Potts, by mistake, rammed the cartridge home ball first. The command was given to fire, but no explosion followed, strange to say. After the engagement, which ended

in the rebels being shelled from their stronghold, an examination took place, when the above circumstance was disclosed. On questioning Potts he laid the blame on the ignorance of his companion, and by that means both got clear.

But to return to our expedition. We sailed to Hog Island (which by the way was not a very poetic cognomen), shortly after sunset, without accident. We retired, leaving an examination for the next day. Early in the morning we commenced our explorations. Hog Island is about seven miles in length and contains about fifteen families, it is about seventeen miles from the mainland. The inhabitants are rather illiterate, very few knowing how to read or write, but hospitable. My host and hostess were the richest family on the island, and treated me very kindly. The host, whose name was Wm. Doughty, followed the sea for his living, leaving the cares of the small farm upon which he resided to his wife and daughters, who are well fitted for the task.

Most of the inhabitants hunt for their living, selling their game to the wealthier inhabitants of the mainland. They fill up the intervals by going "clamming and oystering," supplying vessels with these products of their labor. This war has sadly interfered with their employment, few vessels having stopped at the place since the war broke out. The beach is covered with shells of which I secured some specimens. It is considered one of the most dangerous coasts on the continent, many vessels having been lost with all on board on the sand shoals which line the waters in this vicinity. Remains of wrecks are seen strewn over the beach and high and dry above the sea looms up the framework of a steamer's walking beam. It is imbedded firmly in the sand, and strange to say has never been touched by the inhabitants for firewood. In many a house I saw the boards on which the name of vessels are usually painted, nailed over the fireplace as a relic of some boat that has been wrecked off this coast.

Perhaps a description of my hostess would interest some of your readers of the fair sex. Unlike most of the women on this island, whose pinched features tell of a hard winter, Mrs. Doughty was the picture of health and good living. Just imagine a woman weighing three hundred pounds, with a countenance built on the same scale of liberality, and wearing No. 13 brogans, to which she made constant references, and you have her. But if her body was large so was her heart, and a better souled person I never met. Her table literally groaned beneath the food piled upon it. Woe to the person who had no appetite when he sat down to her table, for he had to eat whether or not he had an appetite. Words fail to convey the kindness with which I was treated while there.

Wild game abounds on the waters; brant being considered the best. They are a species of duck, nearly as large as a goose before being picked. I saw flocks over a mile in length and so thick they could scarcely be told from the clouds. The oysters which are taken from the bay are very good, indeed, being saltier than those we have up North, although not as large. The inhabitants of the island are all strong Union people; the only "secesh" the place ever produced being the former light house keeper. He fled at the beginning of the troubles. The people are strong abolitionists. I did not see a negro on the whole island. But my paper is full so I must close for the present. I will finish in my next.
S.H.B., Jr.

Poughkeepsie Eagle May 9, 1862
We had the pleasure of shaking hands with our friend Lieut. Stephen H. Bogardus of Company H, Purnell Legion, which was encamped when he left on Druid Hill Park, about eight miles from the city of Baltimore. He is here on a short furlough, which he says was not very easy to obtain about this time, although his sister lay dangerously sick at the time he obtained off. We are glad to say she is now better. The lieutenant is looking hearty and rugged as his best friends could wish.

Poughkeepsie Daily Eagle

[NEUTRAL IN NOTHING.]

Camp Van Buren, Baltimore, Md.
Tuesday, May 20th, 1862

Dear Eagle:

We are now in the midst of summer, and the season of flowers. Epicures may envy us, for since the destruction of the Merrimac and the capture of Norfolk the market is blessed with strawberries and green peas. Our encampment is located in a beautiful place. It was originally laid out to sell to the city of Baltimore for a cemetery, but was not purchased. Consequently no trouble was taken to keep it in repair, but still enough of its former loveliness to make it a delightful resort for picnics and dining parties.

Separated by a fine stream of water are several small villages, whose livelihood is in the manufactories that line the banks of the aforementioned stream. The girls of these villages are the magnet that attracts many of our boys to their residences, in spite of vigilant guard or a guardhouse with its concomitants. It is an old proverb that "Love laughs at locksmiths", and so does he at the regulations of the U.S. army.

We, that is the 6th regiment, furnish a guard for the two National Hospitals in this city. It came my turn to be officer of the guard at those places last Wednesday. I was very much gratified to see everything look so clean and nice. While I was there several committees from various states called to see about the wounded of their respective states. They unanimously agreed with me in the opinion that they had never seen establishments of the kind kept in such good order. The patients seemed quite comfortable too. The ladies of Baltimore are constantly sending in delicacies.

While I was there a detachment of wounded rebels were sent there from jail. They were captured at Pittsburgh and Williamsport. A more wretched, squalid looking set of men I never laid eyes upon. You might search Five Points through most minutely and you could not find any to surpass these samples of the boasted "chivalry of the South." They belonged to the 24th and 28th Virginia, 14th Louisiana, and 5th North Carolina regiments. If there was any difference the Virginia regiments were the worst looking as well as the most impudent and loud-mouthed in execration of the detested Yankees. I suppose they were F.F.V.'s of course.

The uniform for the officers (for we had two lieutenants in the apartment) and men seemed to be the same course homespun which our paupers would refuse to wear, plentifully decked with patches. The contrast between their demeanor and that of our federal soldiers was marked. While our troops bore with fortitude their pangs, scarcely allowing a groan to pass them; the secesh made the night hideous with their cries and lamentations. Could it have been the difference in constitutions or was the conscience at work? Some of them said they were forced into the service, while others boasted their treasonous sentiments in the face of death. One thing speaks volumes: Every one that dies, ere their eyes close in death has taken the oath of allegiance. They were born under the government and seem unwilling to die under any other, although they have been fighting against it and have received a death wound in the struggle.
S.H.B. Jr.

𝔓𝔬𝔲𝔤𝔥𝔨𝔢𝔢𝔭𝔰𝔦𝔢 𝔇𝔞𝔦𝔩𝔶 𝔈𝔞𝔤𝔩𝔢

[NEUTRAL IN NOTHING.]

Harper's Ferry,
June 1st, 1862

Dear Eagle:

The "first rose of summer" has bloomed in this most historic and scenic place in the Union. But Harper's Ferry in 1852 and Harper's Ferry in 1862 are vastly different places. The former a blossom in the wilderness, and the latter a ruin. Nature looks the same in every atom. The weather is fine, but man has caused all the difference. Where once was a flourishing little town naught is left to show the passer by but ruin and deserted homes. This morning but one family could be found in town although they are now returning one by one.

But I suppose your readers would prefer to hear of my adventures since I left the Monumental City for Harper's Ferry. We left camp at 12 o'clock and reached the depot at 1 P.M., we were to leave at 2 P.M. Two o'clock came, and three, but still we remained at the depot. Well, to cut a long story short, we got off precisely at 9 P.M., just seven hours after the fixed time. We were crowded like cattle in baggage cars and moved at a snail's pace along toward our destination. At length the sweet restorer, sleep, descended on us. About 5 A.M. I woke and beheld a glorious scene — the sun was just rising over the mountains, gilding everything around. The dewdrops glistened like diamonds, a small stream along the line of the road mingled the music of it's turbid waters with the strains of the birds. I altered my look to the car and what a contrast was there. Without all peace, within men whose trade was war. Some too were going to fight their own relatives, for many of them will find relations in the Maryland Battalion under Jackson.

Well, we arrived without accident at the Maryland side of Harper's Ferry. None of our baggage had managed to keep pace and we were told to make ourselves comfortable. A fine prospect surely. Nice soft slate stones for feathers and Heavens for covering. We got through it somehow, although our bones ached. A good breakfast which I got in the village soon set me right.

About 2 P.M. we started for the Virginia side where we arrived in about fifteen minutes and immediately marched to the armory to exchange our old altered muskets for serviceable arms. We got Austrian rifles, Minie muskets, and Remington rifles with sabre bayonets. We then marched for about two miles and halted for the night. About midnight we were awakened, but it proved to be nothing but a false alarm. The next day part of our brigade went out on a reconnaissance, and we supposed we were to support them. In the afternoon we received orders to march, and supposed the time had come to avenge the 1st Maryland — but the day was not yet. We fell back and formed in battle array.

The artillery opened and was answered, but the rebels fell short — we soon silenced one of their batteries. But that was all they did — their infantry did not support the artillery. However we waited anxiously for the enemy but they did not come — and well for us they did not, for one battery on the banks of the Shenandoah would have rendered our position untenable. Night descended with her sable robes around us and found us watching. About 9 A.M. orders were received to fall back, which we did, leaving everything, even to our camp chest.

We fell back to an eminence on Bolivar Heights, the same ground that had been occupied by the rebels a year ago under Johnston. Here we were secure against all the force Jackson could bring. We threw up entrenchments and waited. About five o'clock that evening the ball opened. It had been raining all day; the ground was muddy and the heavens cloudy. Suddenly a flash lighted up the whole horizon and our "Baby Waker," as we called the large Dahlgren gun from the Maryland heights, opened on the "confeds" with a roar that shook the whole heights. Then both our small batteries joined in the song, and the fighting began.

I went out on the front stoop of Johnston's late headquarters and viewed the whole of it. I saw one act in the play that made me laugh heartily. A company of cavalry was drawn up in a line of battle on the brow of a hill that had been occupied by the 111th Penn. V. and Reynold's Battery U.S.A., the day before when one of the Parrot guns of the above mentioned battery threw a shell in their midst; you should have seen the rebels skedaddle. As they scattered another shell headed them off, and they disappeared over the hill. This gave an interval for a short time between the acts. About twelve o'clock we had another false alarm in which some of our men were slightly wounded by our own men.

Two hours elapsed, when boom went one of the Parrots again, and the second act commenced. Out spoke the Baby Waker, and now over all rang the clarion voice of our old Major Simpson, "fire by file, battalion ready, commence firing". Now the music of the bullet, and the crack of the rifle, played an accompaniment to the play. But "cease firing" soon stopped the performance. Another actor stepped upon the stage. The heavy cannonading had started the cord that bound the clouds, and they were emptying their contents upon us.

But I am wearying your readers with the tedious details. We have had no more fighting at present. This is the first day on which we have had a chance to rest. Truly today is to us a Sabbath, for it is a day of rest. For one week have we been without a night's rest. You men who sit around your firesides and think patriotism is a fine thing, and that the approval of your own conscience is reward enough, ought to stand out under the pelting of a merciless rain, with a wary and vigilant enemy around you, night after night, and live on government rations, viz; salt pork and hard crackers, and only one meal a day at that. I do not wish to boast, but I do not believe any part of the army has undergone greater privations than our "Home Guard", that refused (so the papers said) to go out of the state.

More orders. "Capt. Boyle will muster his company for marching with blankets and six days rations, and deposit their knapsacks in the Quartermaster's tent" is the purport of an order that has just come from headquarters. Ha, we are going to follow Stonewall up, I see. Hurrah for Winchester!

I must close, as you will see by this. More from Winchester I hope.
Yours & c.
S.H.B., Jr.

Poughkeepsie Daily Eagle

[NEUTRAL IN NOTHING.]

Winchester, Va.
June 8, 1862

Dear Eagle:
 'Tis Sunday again and I thought a letter from me would be acceptable even if it was written on the Sabbath. This is a fine place, but I have been visiting a scene that made me feel the horrors of war more than ever. It was the battlefield where Col. Kenly and his brave associates showed their devotion to the old Union. I only made a casual inspection and could secure no memento, as the ground had already been searched over. Several dead horses lay around tainting the air with the stench arising from their decaying flesh.

 About three quarters of a mile from the battlefield is a burying ground of the rebels who were killed in the first capture of Winchester and those who were killed here three weeks ago today. All was quiet with the exception of visitors who were exploring the field. What a different sight was enacted here three weeks ago — the shrill whistle of the bullet, the crack of the rifle, the boom of the cannon, and the whiz of the shell mingled with the shriek and groan of the dying, the fierce neighing of the horses and the hoarse shouts of the officers, must have made a scene that would have needed Hogarth or Rubens to delineate. But such sights are everyday occurrences at present.

 I visited the burying ground where the rebels are buried. There must be over two hundred bodies buried there. Of those killed in the last section the 21st North Carolina seemed to have suffered the most. There are men of Louisiana, Georgia, Tennessee, North Carolina and Virginia, but none of the state of South Carolina. Oh no! It would not do for the patrician blood of the rattlesnake to be shed in defence of her miserable victim Virginia. Bitterly indeed do the rebel prisoners (of whom we have about 200) speak of the South Carolinians and Georgians. They say they are cowards in every sense of the word. I wonder if the mothers, daughters and sisters of the sunny South think of those who are here in the Old Dominion while they for whom they are fighting are far away, laughing in their sleeves at their deluded victims who have paid for their folly with their lives. What punishment should be meted out to those who have revolutionized the best and happiest government in the world, caused the best blood of America to flow like water, and make the finest places in the Union mere deserts. No fate could be too hard for them. But as the saying is, "soldiers have nothing to do with morals," so I suppose they have nothing to do with moralizing.

  I have been in jail to see the rebel prisoners — they are mostly Marylanders, Virginians and Louisianians. They are a better looking set of men than are generally seen in the Southern army. Among them is a boy, (for I can call him nothing else) 15 years old, who wears sergeant's stripes — he has been in service thirteen months. He is a native of New York who had been going to school in Virginia, and I suppose the excitement made him volunteer. He was not impressed into service but came voluntarily. His name is Byron Lee and he lived in Cambridge, Washington County. He is very anxious to hear from home, as he has not heard from his friends since he has been soldiering. If this meets his friends' eyes they will know were he is.

  A great many of the prisoners wish to take the Oath of Allegiance, but some are as full of fight as ever. They are all very sociable and as full of brag as ever — they think a good deal of Jackson. The greater part of them fought at the battle of Bull

Run, and boast a great deal of their performance. They all agree that the best fighting on the ground by our troops was by the Fire Zouaves. One man belonging to a Mississippi regiment said they cut his corps all to pieces and not fifty escaped. I secured in this place several trophies, among which is a small silk secesh flag with the word Dixie worked in the centre.

Hark! Music is stealing softly in at the window. 'Tis the band of the 60th N.Y.S.V. who are playing for church. By the by, I almost forgot to mention one thing. Among the officers of the 78th N.Y.S.V. is Lieut. Allen, son of A. L. Allen of Po'keepsie, an old schoolmate of mine. At present he is on Gen. Slough's staff. We found a great many things that may be called trophies, belonging as they did to the "Confeds." In fact this paper on which this letter is written may be called contraband as I confiscated it, to use the military term, in the office of a lawyer who, judging from the papers found there, must have been a Quartermaster in some rebel regiment. If I had not found it I could not have written this letter, for my trunk, together with all the baggage belonging to the brigade, is still in Harper's Ferry.

While I am writing this a detachment of four hundred rebel prisoners have just passed by my window and are to be followed by another batch of 500. I understand several New Yorkers are found among them. Oh! I forgot to tell you this letter is written in the sanctum of the editor of the Winchester Republican. My company is quartered in the building and are making themselves at home. But the men are around to get passes for church and I must close.

Yours & c.
S.H.B., Jr.

𝕻𝖔𝖚𝖌𝖍𝖐𝖊𝖊𝖕𝖘𝖎𝖊 𝕯𝖆𝖎𝖑𝖞 𝕰𝖆𝖌𝖑𝖊

[NEUTRAL IN NOTHING.]

Camp Goodrich, Near Strasburg, Va.
June 25th, 1862

Dear Eagle:

Here in the midst of Nature's solitude I pen these few lines. Since last I indited a letter to you I have traveled many a weary mile. On Friday night, June 18th, Cos. G. and F. received orders to go, in company with detachments of other regiments, to a place called Snicker's Ferry, a small place on the Shenandoah about fifteen miles from Winchester and fourteen from Berryville. We stayed at that place until last Wednesday, when we returned to Winchester, and found that the brigade under command of Gen. Slough had gone to Middletown, about sixteen miles further. Next morning we started for that place where we arrived at noon. We remained there until yesterday, when expecting an attack from Jackson's forces we advanced to this place, about four miles from our last encampment.

We have here or in this vicinity, Gen. Fremont, Banks, Sigel, Schenk and Milroy, with Shields and McDowell in supporting distance. The number of troops I will not state. One thing, however, you and the others would be astonished to hear the number. The Generals most feared by the rebels are Shields and Sigel. Put citizen's clothes on the latter and no one would recognize the hero of Pea Ridge in the plain, unassuming man before you. But examine him closely; watch that eye and compressed lip with its occasional twitching, and you have a slight index to that brain which, working night and day, controls our movements.

The casual reader may look at the Army bulletin for the movements before Richmond, but not until Jackson is defeated will the rebel Capital be ours. The Confederate troops, with the immense supplies cut off that are in this valley, will be as children in the hands of the Federals. Starve or fight will be their alternatives, and if they should gain a victory, which we do not for one instant suppose possible, are they any better situated? No! for the grain would be all gone and there is nothing to take its place.

Probably there is no prettier place in the world for scenery. Yesterday I took a stroll around to see the country— about two miles from here we stopped at a house and went on the front stoop to view the prospect. Parallel with the garden fence flowed Cedar Creek, muddy and swollen from recent rains, while directly in front of us, seemingly from the Blue Ridge, rushed the blue waters of the North Branch of the Shenandoah, commonly called the North River. For miles the waters of the two streams flowed as separate and distinct as when they flowed in their natural beds. The same phenomena is observed at Harpers Ferry for a short distance, where the Shenandoah and Potomac join. Over the majestic mountains towered, displaying various lights and shadows as the sun seemed to sport among them, while their summits pierced the clouds. At their foot runs the Strasburg and Front Royal Railroad, and just visible in the distance was Manassas Gap.

Along the line of the railroad were a few dwellings that peered through the tree tops as peacefully as though the War Fiend had never set his foot on this once happy land. It was over this railroad that part of Beauregard's reinforcements came on that memorable Sabbath when our troops again baptized in blood the Stars and Stripes. Probably over this road some of our soldiers came as prisoners. Foolish indeed would have been the Federal soldier who one year ago attempted to ramble through this peaceful vale as it seems.

  I was conversing with a once wealthy inhabitant of this neighborhood. He owns 1,500 acres of land which one year ago was worth $100 per acre. Now he has not enough to keep himself and family for a month. And he is several miles away from the main road. For months he has not tasted coffee or sugar, and has seen no papers since the 6th of March. Think of that, you who have your coffee enlivened by the morning paper and wonder whether these men had their senses or were insane. He, in common with the other sufferers in this region, now wail their losses which they charge upon the war, while they seem to forget who called up the spirit which now devastates their property. They curse South Carolina for making them do the fighting at home. The extreme Southerners did not see the beauty of doing the fighting on their soil as long as the Border States could be made to do it. But the Border States are getting their eyes opened and the play is nearly ended. Probably the next letter I write will be after a severe battle, as we expect one every day.
Yours & c.
S.H.B., Jr.

𝔓𝔬𝔲𝔤𝔥𝔨𝔢𝔢𝔭𝔰𝔦𝔢 𝔇𝔞𝔦𝔩𝔶 𝔈𝔞𝔤𝔩𝔢

[NEUTRAL IN NOTHING.]

In Camp, Near Warrenton, Va.
July 13th, 1862

Dear Eagle:

Since I last wrote you I have traveled many long miles and changed my location several times. We left Camp Goodrich, near Middletown, July 5th, and arrived here Friday last about 10 A.M. If any of your readers will get a Campaign Map they can see the distance. The Fourth was celebrated by us at Camp Goodrich by the booming of cannon at the break of day, and at Meridan, Gen. Cooper reviewed the division at 10 A.M. and delivered a few soul stirring remarks to us. In the evening the officers belonging to the 2nd Brigade called on Col. Talt of the 1st District of Columbia Volunteers, acting Brigadier General, with the band belonging to the 60th N.Y.S.V., and gave him a serenade. We were invited in and stayed till the "wee sma' hours" warned us it was time to go.

The next evening we were plodding our weary way toward Front Royal. That night we slept in the woods with no covering over us but Heaven's blue and boundless canopy. We reached Front Royal Sunday noon, tired out with our tedious but not long march. Front Royal, like the other places through which we have passed, abounds in trees, fruit, flowers and secessionists. I do not believe there is a single Union inhabitant in the place. The fact is the place is almost deserted, very few living here at present. The village has but one street, and along that it stretches for half a mile.

We left Front Royal Wednesday morning at 6 A.M. and arrived at a place called Washington at 8 P.M., traveling over 25 miles. This was the longest and hardest day's march we had since we left Baltimore, and in consequence our path was marked with stragglers all along the route. It was a very hot day and the road was very rough. Washington is a town nearly as large as Winchester, but not near so business-like looking. It contains three good sized hotels but very few stores.

The road over which we came is dotted here and there by the mansions of the F.F.V.'s whose business is raising slaves for the southern market. We did not stay in this place very long, as it was discovered that we were about six miles out of the way and had to recover that distance and make nine more. This we thought lightly of, and marched on, passing Bank's division on the way. Mile after mile was then passed over; the last was out of sight in the rear and yet we did not stop. The Blue Ridge had been crossed and we were near the Rappahannock River.

The country was different from that through which we had passed. No water was to be found, and we were looking for it before we could encamp. "Have you any water in your canteens?" is asked, and the mournful answer "No!" is heard along the whole column. Surely there will be water in that ravine, but when we get there none is to be found. Not a house is to be seen; all the cultivation is the rail fences along the route. Soon an aide rides down the line stating that water was to be found three miles ahead. Three more miles to be traversed by sore feet, aching heads and bodies and weary limbs. Three more miles to be walked by our men almost ready to drop from fatigue. Nearly twenty miles have been marched by us and three more to be marched. Nearly twenty miles have been traversed over from 10 A.M., and 'tis nearly 8 P.M. and yet three miles are to be traveled before we can rest. But such reflections will not make the distance any shorter, so cheer up, three miles are not so very long after all. Soon the welcome command to halt is given and we stop. Half of the men fall to the ground and in a few minutes are in the land of dreams.

You rich who dress in purple and fine linen, and fare sumptuously every day, what would you give for the peaceful sleep of the dusty soldier, whose fare is a cup of coffee and hard crackers while on a march? No conscience troubles him, and he awakes in the morning from his hard couch with no covering over him, refreshed; while you arise from your sleepless pillow of down with aching head and feverish brow.

We remained here till daylight next morning, when we fell in and arrived at this place, as I said before, about 10 A.M. We are about 8 miles from Warrenton, and as far as the eye can reach are the tents of Pope's Grand Army of Virginia. Do not think, however, I mean we are all together, but a regiment here and a battery there, till they reach the other side of Warrenton. This country is not as fruitful as in the Valley of Virginia. Sterile fields and stunted trees have taken place of waiving grain and beautiful cottages with their appurtenances.

We are now in Farquair county, about midway between Alexandria and Gordonsville. One thing, however, is produced here in abundance, viz. horses. This article is of the finest stock, and our division has its share of contrabands. A great many of the men when tired out with our long marches would go to the field and take a horse which they would ride to our destination and at night loose him, and the sagacious animal would find its way home.

But a new direction is given to my thoughts as I hear some band playing a dead march. Some regiment is burying a fellow member. Who he is I do not know, but still he is a brother soldier and I think perhaps I may be the next victim. There is nothing so sublimely beautiful as a soldier's funeral. The sweet, though mournful strains, and the sad, slow march of the

soldiers, make one feel there is something in Death. The firing over the grave by the detail closes the scene and the soldier is returned to his former dust.
Yours & c.,
S.H.B., Jr.

Poughkeepsie Daily Eagle

[NEUTRAL IN NOTHING.]

In Camp, Near Warrenton, Va.
July 31st, 1862

Dear Eagle:

You would have heard from me ere this had it not been for illness. I have been near to the gates of death, and I am writing this not because I am really able, but am exhausted lying on my back for nearly a fortnight. We left our camp near Warrenton on Friday the 18th for this place, but in consequence of rain halted at a place called Waterloo. That night I saw a magnificent scene— the streams had so swollen that as far as the eye could reach the road was under water. Part of the supply train that we were guarding had got about a mile ahead of us and were cut off by the water from returning or going forward. With the exception of five wagons, whose teams were saved, the train was driven up a steep hill out of the reach of the water. The five before mentioned were completely covered and in the morning one floated off, the top bursting and strewing the water with clothing. Jackets, pants and under-clothes floated around, vainly seeking for takers but none came.

Gen. Banks and staff were caught too and pitched their tents on the summit of the same hill. Four companies of the 60th N.Y., just from Harper's Ferry, were with him without any tents. Fortunately our men had that afternoon received their new shelter tents and were comparatively comfortable. To add to the beauty of the scene a large mill that had been used for making army cloth for the rebels had been set on fire and the light it made could be seen for miles around. Here we stayed till Monday. We could have gone before but a corps of military carpenters were engaged at putting up a bridge over Hedgeman's River by which we could save a day's journey. The original bridge had been destroyed by the rebels in the retreat from Manassas to cut off McClellan's pursuit. It was, for the secesh, labor thrown away.

We reached Little Washington the same afternoon and pitched our tents. Here we stayed three or four days when we moved our camp to this place. We are doing nothing out of the usual routine of camp life. Our Provost Guard has the most duty to do guarding the houses and property around the country. Day before yesterday General Banks reviewed the troops comprising his Corps de Armes. I was too unwell to witness it but those who saw it said it was a splendid sight. Troops representing nearly 100,000 men were there. After the review came Division and Brigade drill — cavalry charged upon the infantry whose glistening bayonets drove them back, while the artillery played incessantly. Probably it was one of the best sham battles ever fought.

We are anxiously awaiting the order to advance. We can whip Jackson, but while we are waiting here another enemy is decimating our ranks faster than all the guerrillas between here and Richmond. Disease, fell, insidious disease is eating the vitals of the army and counting its victims by the thousands. Out of 3,000 comprising this brigade at Harper's Ferry only 269 turned out for the review on Tuesday. What causes it I do not know. Vegetables however are very much needed. Salt pork and hard crackers may do for cold weather, but then it produces all kinds of disease at present.

We are getting fresh meat every alternate day but seldom any vegetables and never any soft bread. I do not think it the fault of any of the officers commanding the department, but I suppose the Sanitary Commissions at home think of nobody but the army before Richmond. Another grievance is that the men are not able to purchase anything for themselves because they are not paid off regular. One regiment in the brigade were paid off last week for the first time since the organization which was nearly ten months ago. This regiment has not been paid off for just five months and the men need the funds for their families if not for themselves. Now this is a wrong that should be immediately remedied. I hope some of our philanthropic societies will occasionally think there is an army of the valley of Virginia that would like some of their attention. Men cannot fight while they are sick or those at home are suffering.

I received to-day a sprightly little paper published at Warrenton by the members of the 9th N.Y.S.M. who are doing Provost Guard at that place. It is about half the size of the Daily Eagle. It contains nothing but local news. It is published at the old office of the Warrenton Whig, a secession sheet. The 9th will soon purify the establishment.

Yours & c.,

S.H.B., Jr.

Poughkeepsie Daily Eagle

[NEUTRAL IN NOTHING.]

Kadysville, Md.,
Sept. 19, 1862

Dear Eagle:
 After a lapse of many weeks I have found an opportunity to write a few lines. The smoke of the battle of Wednesday has not yet cleared away, still we can see enough to know that Little Mac has gained another victory. I had, together with my Regiment, the honor to participate in the fray. Tuesday night we arrived on the left, but at ten P.M. were ordered to march to the right. All night the pickets and skirmishers were firing upon each other — but the ball did not open till daylight. Then the artillery commenced playing, and in a few moments the roar of cannon and the rattle of musketry, combined with the groans and shrieks of the wounded and dying, made a scene that cannot be put on paper.
 About 7 A.M. our brigade was ordered forward as the first reserve. The boys went willingly, although they had had nothing to eat since the night before. In a little while we were ordered to advance and enter into action. At a double quick we marched to the conflict. We were on the right under Hooker — "Fighting Joe" as he is called. We were ordered to take the cornfield and support the 124th Pennsylvania Volunteers, a new regiment, which we did till about noon. That cornfield was a horrible sight. A live rebel soldier is a disgusting sight, but a dead one surpasses description. And that field was full of them, lying

in all positions. Here, one shot through the heart; there, one with his leg torn off; and still farther on, a trunk without a head.

At noon we were sent to a piece of woods on the advance of the right — and here we remained till about 2 P.M., at which time I was wounded and carried to the rear. I was hit by a musket ball coming from a party of rebels carrying our flag. This was the second time I saw the same treachery during the battle. What the world thinks of a foe that in the disguise of a friend shoots you down, I know not; but it seems to be their style of fighting. Our forces have captured a great number of rebel battle flags, while I think we lost none. Our loss in wounded is almost innumerable, but in killed small in proportion. The rebel loss in killed far exceeds ours, but in wounded I think not. This is accounted for by the rebels using the old buck and ball, while our boys use Minie balls altogether, and they kill when they hit. I was shot off my horse and lost him. But we whipped them — and I would give another horse for such a victory.
Yours & c.,
S.H.B., Jr.

[We learn that Acting Adjutant Bogardus was severely wounded in the mouth. He arrived here last evening by the Mary Powell. We hope his wound is not serious.]

Poughkeepsie Daily Eagle

[NEUTRAL IN NOTHING.]

Bolivar Heights, Va.
Sunday, Nov. 9, 1862

Dear Eagle:

    I hope neither you nor my friends thought I was dead, for if so, you and they will be sadly disappointed to find I am still here — waiting for "something to turn up". I have been here now two weeks, and during that time have experienced several types of weather. I arrived here during a rain; last Sunday was as warm as a summer's day, and at present it is as cold as December. The storm extended to us, but the snow has almost disappeared from the ground.

    This morning part of this Brigade went out on a reconnaissance in force in the direction of Charlestown. This place is where John Brown and his misguided associates expiated their crimes. We passed through it last spring. But how the country has been desolated since last May! Where our camp now stands, was part of a wood which then extended for several miles— now the vision reaches over a cleared plain to the range of mountains in the distance; and Bolivar, then a place of some importance, is the Deserted Village of Goldsmith — if not in truth, at least in resemblance.

    But Harper's Ferry — the Mecca of the south — what can be said of it? Alas! It will never regain its pristine splendor. Like a diamond in a beautiful setting, it sat among the hills which clustered around it, the loveliest among thousands. Now ruins greet the eye, whichever way it turns; and but for the sol-

diers which dot the place, and the rumble of government teams, the place would seem more like a graveyard than of so much importance as the "Key of Washington" should be. When we marched up this road last May, we passed a graveyard, around which was a tasty railing. What a change has come over the scene! Every picket has disappeared and on one of the gateposts, which still remain, some sacrilegious officer has tacked an advertisement of horses for sale. Still it is used as a graveyard— not by the inhabitants of this vicinity— for there are none left— but by the army. Here lies all that is mortal of many a brave soldier who left his home to give his life in defence of his country's flag — not, perhaps on the battle field, for diseases of the camp are more fatal than the shot or shell.
Yours, & c.
S.H.B., Jr.

Poughkeepsie Daily Eagle

[NEUTRAL IN NOTHING.]

Headquarters, Purnell Legion, Frederick City, Md.
Jan. 31, 1863

Dear Eagle:

    I have waited, like Micawber, for "something to turn up." But still everything moves along in the old track. What a dearth of news, and a war in progress that engages the attention of the whole world! This city, which contains about 8,000 inhabitants, was the great hospital for the wounded of Antietam. The United States Hotel and the principal churches and public buildings were turned into hospitals. For the last two weeks the Government has been emptying everything but two Government Hospital Camps and one barracks.

    When we first came here the streets, on a pleasant afternoon, were filled with convalescent wounded soldiers. The bandaged head, the empty sleeve, and the stump of a leg, told a tale louder than words could speak. Those who spoke flippantly of patriotism as a mere word should have seen some of those that I have met. I have seen men now in this army who are hardly able to carry a gun or bestride a horse. 'Tis easy to talk about dying for one's country when sitting at your fireside, but to do it is an entirely different thing. You may say, 'tis very easy for you to talk thus, who are situated so pleasantly. We are, in truth, very well fixed for the first time in many a long day, and on that account can appreciate it the better. We live well, don't have anything of consequence to do, and are getting lazy, even for a soldier.

The force here, and in the neighborhood, consists of the 3d Delaware, Rush's Lancers and our Regt. At the city, and the 14th New Jersey at Monocacy Junction. We now belong to the 8th Corps and are under Gen. Schenk. There is a large sprinkling of negroes in the population, and it's majority are or were slaves, their looks denote that their masters were practically in favor of amalgamation. Some of these negroes have become very insolent of late, and only last week one of them came very near his death from a sentinel he had insulted.

We had a visit from the Paymaster this week — a person who is always welcome. We have been favored, having been paid up to New Years. To make him come often we gave him an oyster supper.

Some two weeks ago I made a visit to Baltimore, and while there went to see the 150th. They have improved a great deal in drill and discipline under Lieut. Colonel Bartlett. They bid fair to rival the best regiment in service, and excel a great many.

About the only excitement we have is occasionally a raid from rebel cavalry that is in the neighborhood of Loudon County, Virginia. Several attempts have been made to break up this organization, which rejoices in the nomenclature of White's Independent Cavalry; but they have only partially succeeded. The great advantages a body of men like this have, is their knowledge of the country, and their easy disbanding, to meet again at short notice. Several of them, including officers, have been captured at Harper's Ferry lately, since which they have been less daring. The boys would like a little excitement of that kind, to keep their blood from stagnating in the veins.

Last week a number of rebels were sent away from the hospital to Baltimore, having been paroled. They had been wounded and captured at South Mountain and Antietam. They came ragged and dirty — but they left here in new uniforms, furnished by their friends and sympathizers in the city. I have

myself seen finely dressed ladies with their arms full of clothing for the wounded rebels. This may be all right, but I can't see it. The rebels would not allow the Union people of the south to treat our men thus.
Yours,
S.H.B., Jr.

Poughkeepsie Daily Eagle

[NEUTRAL IN NOTHING.]

Headquarters, Purnell Legion, Frederick City, Md.,
Feb. 16, 1863

Dear Eagle:
    'Tis a fine morning more like April than February; but there is one great drawback to pleasure on such a morning here, it is the ruling article of the south, viz. mud. You at home cannot imagine it, unless you have seen it. Get off of the paved road, and your horse can hardly wade through, even when unencumbered except by his rider. Government teams are doubled, and then can scarcely move along at a snail's pace.
    I saw an extract from a letter written to you by Benson J. Lossing, in the Baltimore American of last week, about which I wish to speak without offending the author. He speaks of the good effect of officers' wives and sisters in camp. I agree with him, except that it is not always practicable. In a city like Baltimore, or even here, it is very easy, and some of our officers have followed the example. But what would women do on a march? There are no conveyances for the sick when we travel, and what could or would our better halves do to journey 20 or 30 miles a day! And I have not mentioned anything about scarcity of food. Why, on our retreat from Manassas, during the memorable September, the whole army was without food for days at a time, and glad to get cracker. What then would have been the situation of those upon whom we would not have the rough wind blow or the rain moisten? After a battle, none so good as woman can be found; but must they endure all the privations and hardships simply to nurse us? Camp is not a place for woman, as my little

experience teaches me. They are the subjects of coarse jests among the men and many a word reaches their ears which causes the blood to mantle their faces as modesty is wounded.

Last Thursday night quite a laughable accident occurred in this city. About eight o'clock P.M. a body of cavalry was heard coming down the Hagerstown turnpike. None of our troops were expected and the exclamation of "The Confederates are coming", was in every body's mouth. Secesh was jubilant, and Union people looked anxious. Great was the uproar in town. However, the cavalry reached the city and proved to be a detachment of the 1st Maryland Cavalry, on their way to join their regiment at Harper's Ferry. When it was found out who they were a great change was seen in the countenances of the citizens. The faces of the rebel sympathizers were very sensibly elongated, while the friends of the Union were joking them about Stuart's Cavalry. *Moral: Don't halloo till you are out of the woods.*

I hear that the rebel cavalry in the neighborhood of Harper's Ferry and Winchester is being gradually broken up by capture and death. It is a small force, but being natives of that country they are well acquainted with the ground on which our forces are and can do a great deal of damage to us. However, nearly all of their officers are captured or killed and indeed Jeff Davis' retaliatory proclamation will probably remain in durance vile for some time.

The unusually warm winter is good for the soldiers on the Rappahannock but we have had some terrible storms of wind and rain.

Yours,

S.H.B., Jr.

Poughkeepsie Daily Eagle

[NEUTRAL IN NOTHING.]

Headquarters Purnell Legion, Md Vols., Frederick City, Md.
March 1, 1863

Dear Eagle:
    Although 'tis Sunday evening and the church bells are ringing, still I must either write to-night or not at all. Not that the Sabbath is to me a day of leisure, on the contrary all my work has fallen on this day.
Last Saturday being a pleasant day I took the notion of riding down to Harper's Ferry to visit a friend— Lieut. Brouner, formerly of the 5th New York, but who is now Adjutant of the 7th Maryland. On mentioning the subject to our surgeon he agreed to accompany me. We mounted our horses and started. The day was beautiful and the roads pretty good and we promised ourselves a very pleasant ride.
    The country through which we passed is a very pretty landscape and well settled. It shows throughout the signs of war, viz. Desolation — although in a very small degree. We arrived without any accident at the Ferry. The place seemed more forlorn than usual. I found my friend's regiment was encamped on Maryland Heights. The Doctor and I here parted, he going over the Ferry to see some friends, while I took my journey Heavenward. I arrived at my destination about 2 o'clock P.M. and was received by Lieut. Brouner with many hand shakings. As it was the first meeting since last winter many were the questions and answers that flew between us.

The time passed swiftly away till supper time when I sat down to one of the best suppers I ever ate in camp. Our circle was enlivened by the presence of the wife of one of the officers. We chatted merrily till tattoo sounded, after which we adjourned to the tent of the officer of the day where we had some very fine music. The night was pleasant, but imagine my surprise in the morning on awakening and finding a furious snow storm raging while the ground was deeply covered. Matters did not look very promising for a twenty miles ride, but it was Sunday and as usual important work lay at my tent in Frederick which must be attended to. With many expressions of regret at my short stay and invitations to come again, I mounted my horse who stood impatiently pawing the snow and started for home.

On my descent from the Heights I beheld a most beautiful landscape before me. The snow was falling and the side of the mountain was covered, while at its foot rolled the broad Potomac swelled by the recent rains and the green Shenandoah came rushing down Loudon Heights to meet it, swelling it to a torrent which raised as it rolled toward the Bay. In the distance was Harper's Ferry, its ruins looking like spectres amid the garb of snow which partially covered them, while afar off loomed up Loudon Heights. But such a view must be seen to be appreciated.

I found the Doctor waiting at the foot of the hill for me. He dissuaded me from the attempt to reach Frederick. But neither time, tide, nor the War Department wait for dilatory Adjutants, so all the arguments went to swell the gale that was blowing. Onward we went, but at Knoxville the Doctor found his boots nearly full of snow, we dismounted and went into the hotel. He filled the legs of his boots with paper and started again. The storm was terrible and we were facing it. Every flake seemed an arrow destined for our faces. Still forward we went. "There's a covered bridge a few miles ahead," says the Doctor where we can dismount and warm ourselves. Onward still, onward was not exactly the cry but the action. Soon the welcome bridge hove into sight, and we alighted. For half an hour we went through motions more vigorous than graceful, then mounted and continued our journey.

At a little place called Jefferson we stopped for a dinner for ourselves and our horses. After getting thoroughly warmed we continued our ride. We had heretofore been riding in the valley, we now had to surmount the hills that skirt this city. It was terrible — the wind howled and the snow fell more rapidly, while to add to our troubles the road which had seemed going down was drifted very bad and it was as much as our beasts could do to flounder through it.

But all troubles must have an end — soon the welcome city of Frederick was reached. People stared at us as we rode through the streets as though we were visitors from the other world. And I assure you either of us would have made a good picture to illustrate the month of February. Our hair and whiskers were lumps of ice, while our faces were coated with the same article. But we were home, and a good fire made everything all right again, and we laughed over our adventure. There is nothing stirring in this place in the shape of news. Business is slowly improving and the March winds are drying the roads.

S.H.B., Jr.

Poughkeepsie Daily Eagle

[NEUTRAL IN NOTHING.]

Head Quarters Purnell Md. Vols.
Camp Monocacy, Md.
June 5, 1863

Dear Eagle:

As it is so long since I last wrote that a letter may not be acceptable, but I'll bother you any way.

On Thursday to relieve the monotony of camp life I concluded to visit the old battleground of Antietam. Leaving the City Hotel early in the morning I started for that memorable spot. The day was pleasant and the scenery fine. The road winds through the most beautiful portion of Maryland. We pass South Mountain with different feelings from those that animated our breasts on our first passage. South Mountain Gap has been described by several writers and as we were not actively engaged I will not trouble your readers with a repetition of its beauties. If the artist wishes a view of American scenery the wild gorges, narrow ravines, and precipitous sides of this range of mountains, which I believe are a branch of the Cumberland, would furnish him with a subject, which, faithfully recreated, could not be surpassed.

We arrived at Boonsboro about 8 o'clock A.M. and took breakfast at the United States Hotel, where "mine host" did his best to accommodate us. While the horse was being fed we took a stroll through the village. Several of the Federal troops were buried in the churchyard in this place with handsome headboards, on which all the information necessary for friends is inscribed.

After stopping here about an hour we started for the battlefield, passing through the village of Keedysville. It was at this place I stopped after I received my wound, and I called at my former quarters to see the folks, who appeared very glad to see me. We drove about 3 or 4 miles further and there turned to the right on a byroad leading to the Dunkard's church at which place was the heaviest fighting on the right, and near which I was shot. This byroad was used by the "Copperheads" both in going and retreating from the field, and is still literally paved with their equipments. In this road the Irish Brigade made their famous charge killing the "Greybacks" by scores. I was informed by the landlord of the United States Hotel that they lay in rows and their blood covered the ground. The wall bears marks of the conflicts. But the old church shows where the heaviest fighting took place. One shell went entirely through it leaving a hole at either end through which a large man might crawl with ease. It is also perforated with bullets and solid shot in many places. How it was left standing is a great wonder. The trees surrounding it, for it is in a piece of woods, are nearly all injured more or less. Nearly every one shows the scars of the contest. Many of them have been broken off at the tops, while the ground is still strewn with branches that were shot off in the fight.

I visited the corn field out of which our forces were driven three times before they could hold possession of it. The spot is altered a great deal, the fences being rebuilt and nearly the whole of the field being ploughed up. Even graves, of which several hundred are in the field, have not been secure from the intrusion of the plough. I could hardly recognize the place in which we stood except by going back to the home, and then marching in the direction that never by me to be forgotten 17th of September. In the barn yard where I lost my horse on the other side of the road were three graves of the 20th New York Militia, one of which bore the inscription, Irving B. Pollock on the headboard. I recollect but one of the other names viz. Ploss.

The wood on the right of the corn fields look familiar, the trees shattered and torn by the stroke of the shell or that of the bullet. Very few of the trees in the corn field have any foliage, most being torn asunder or broken off at the top and standing like blasted monuments to mark the spot where "brother raised his hand against brother, and father against son" in deadly conflict. I saw in one grave 100 rebels buried in this place, and the lady of the house said eight thousand soldiers, two thirds of which were Confederates, were buried on the farm. Her house was used for a hospital, the family being away in Pennsylvania, and everything it contained being ruined. The family returned on Friday after the battle and where they left a home of comfort and ease, found it full of wounded and dying soldiers.

I could not help contrasting the scene of the 17th of September and that of yesterday. Nothing to disturb the harmony of nature. The contrast between the whistle of the partridge, the cooing of the dove, or the stroke of the woodman's axe, and the sound of the shell, the wheugh of the Minie ball, the whistle of the bullet, the rush of cannon ball mingled with the shrieks of the wounded, the groans of the dying, and the yell of the yet living combatant was great; too great to be imagined by those who have never experienced it.

The ground is well culled over for relics, and a few bullets and pieces of shell were all I could find. My companion, however, found in the woods the lower jaw of a rebel soldier which he has in his possession.

Our time being limited we did not visit Sharpsburg but deferred that till another time; so getting in our buggy we drove to camp well pleased with our trip and determined if possible to repeat it.

Yours & c,
S.H.B., Jr.

Poughkeepsie Daily Eagle

[NEUTRAL IN NOTHING.]

Headquarters, Purnell Legion Md. Vols., Fort Delaware, Md. Sept. 17th, 1863.

Dear Eagle:

I know of no better way to celebrate the anniversary of the defeat of the rebels on the bloody field of Antietam in 1862, than by writing to you. Although not in the front, still we are in a place nearly as interesting to the historian, it being the depository of the majority of prisoners of war. There are nearly ten thousand of them here, and a motley crew they are — the only pretension to uniform being rags and dirt. The greater part of them work at different kinds of labor on the island, getting pay from the government for so doing. A loud outcry has been lately made by copperhead organs, which was refuted by the statement of the rebel surgeons (of whom there is quite a number) stationed here, over their own signatures.

The water we have on the island is taken from Brandywine Creek, and is brought here daily by means of a water boat. The island is about 80 acres in area, but the Fort itself, which is built on the same plan as Sumter, covers but about five acres. Outside of the fortifications wooden barracks are erected, capable of holding 25,000 persons.

The prisoners have a great deal more privilege than our men are allowed on Belle Island; many of them say they are better treated than when down in Dixie. Many of them want to take the Oath of Allegiance, but it is not allowed, except in clear cases of conscription or extreme youth. Several hundred of them have gone into our army, nearly a whole battery of heavy artillery being composed of "galvanized greybacks" as they are termed.

This place is very healthy with the exception of the portion occupied by the rebels — and that is their own fault. They are filthy in the extreme, it being as much as the Provost Guard can do to keep them anyways decent in consequence of their disgusting habits. We bury from 18 to 20 every day. The government has purchased a lot of ground in New Jersey. Rings, fans, and other articles of small value are manufactured by them for sale among the federal troops at this port.

Saturday afternoon the cornerstone of a chapel for the use of the troops was laid. The sacred performance was under the supervision of the Bishop of Delaware, assisted by Chaplains Paddock and Ray of the Fort. Copies of the prominent papers of the day along with lists of military officials commanding and on duty at the Fort were placed in the cornerstone. All the military under command of Brig. Gen. Schoepf, were present at the ceremony and the band played several sacred airs. Quite a number of ladies did us the honor of coming from Wilmington to be present. The chapel is to be frame and will be done in about a month.

Today being, as I remarked before, the anniversary of the battle of Antietam, in front of my office are two tattered flags, on the folds of which is inscribed "Antietam, Sept. 17, 1862." Our men and officers have been allowed a great deal more liberty than usual by the General commanding.

The eyes of the whole army are watching for indications of the public sentiment regarding the elections to take place this fall. Shall the government be sustained in its efforts to put down the rebellion? Then elect the unconditional Union Ticket and send Vallandigham, Wood, and their accomplices back to their deserved seclusion. If you wish to dishearten the brave men who have gone from you to fight your battles, then elect the ticket which bears upon its face the deadly venom of the copperhead. Keep step to the music of the Union and do not permit any divisions among you to give joy to the rebel cabal at Richmond already dismayed at the prospect ahead of them or leave a loophole for the European enemies of American freedom, with their cursed and devilish neutrality; to crawl through. Maine has nobly responded to the demands and entreaties of the army and shall New York and Ohio prove recreant to the trusts confided in them by the noble defenders of the starry banner? Show an undivided front to the enemies of our country, march overwhelmingly to the ballot box, crushing out copperheads at home as we do secessionists and rebels, and the gallant soldiers will shower blessings upon your heads and your children will in after years thank you.

Yours, & c.

S.H.B., Jr.

Poughkeepsie Daily Eagle

[NEUTRAL IN NOTHING.]

Headquarters, Purnell Legion, Md. Vols., Fort Delaware, Md.
October 24, 1863

Dear Eagle:

    All eyes are turned to the front and nothing very exciting has transpired here; yet I will venture an epistle. The late elections in Pennsylvania and Ohio have wonderfully relieved the minds of the soldiers, who were anxiously awaiting the news. The seed of the woman has bruised the heel of the serpent — woefully indeed is the copperhead wounded. About 100 of "Andy Curtin men" went to the polls from this fort, to exercise their right of suffrage. I presume this hundred was magnified into many thousands from the Army of the Potomac by the copperheads. But how consistent are they? They originally claimed the whole army as Democratic, yet use every effort to prevent the soldiers from voting.

    The election in Maryland comes off next Wednesday and there is considerable excitement in different parts of the state. Two main tickets, and in several Congressional Districts two candidates, are in the field. They both profess to be Union, but the one endorsed by the Legion and styled "Unconditional" is the only real and true one. Henry Winter Davis has no known opposition and will probably be elected by a large majority. In fact, I think the greater part of the ticket throughout the state will be triumphant.

    The news from the army is meager, and with us, very old. The removal of Gen. Rosecrans is the subject of much comment in all quarters. He was supposed by all to have been just the man for the place. Probably it is all right, and we will know soon enough. Today the papers are full of rumors about Gen. Meade; but we have become so accustomed to change in the commandership of the Army of the Potomac, that we do not speculate about it.

We have been sending away more prisoners to Point Lookout, and another steamer is outside, awaiting the next batch. There are about 5,000 prisoners of war here at present, and I think most of them will be sent away. Demolition of the old barracks is already commenced. Our church is progressing rapidly, and will soon be completed. It will be a pretty piece of architecture when finished.

Yesterday we sent away one of our companies (H), to Annapolis, Md., to relieve a company of the 1st E.S. Md. Regiment. It is to do provost duty at that place. We have here convict soldiers as well as political and rebel prisoners. These convicts are called Company Q and have a unique dress coat, being very short-waisted, and a still shorter swallow tail. The collar, cuffs and tail are trimmed with buff, the main portion of the coat being dark blue. G. Edwards Lester, the author and orator, who is confined here, has written a lyric dedicated to Company Q.

I hope the Empire State will not prove recreant to the trust reposed her, but will profit by the lessons taught her by the October elections and elect the Union ticket. Although I am not able to be with you in body, I am with you in spirit.
S.H.B., Jr.

Poughkeepsie Eagle November 3, 1863
Among those of our soldier friends who have recently returned from the seat of war is our occasional correspondent, Lieut. S.H. Bogardus, Jr. He looks well and healthy.

Poughkeepsie Daily Eagle

[NEUTRAL IN NOTHING.]

Headquarters, Purnell Legion, Md. Vols.,
Chapel Point, near Port Tobacco, Md.,
November 27, 1863

Dear Eagle:
    I am not dead yet, but so far out of the way of civilization that I might, without much trouble, imagine myself so. This country is as far as progress, finished about fifty years ago. If you want to see people working with corn-husk collars and rope traces on their cattle, here is the place to come. Perhaps the mode of churning is the most interesting; it is done in a stone preserve jar with an ordinary stick, making about a quart of milk into butter, after churning. Think of the people of this age, living in the midst of a fine agricultural country (for this is one), sending to Baltimore (two days travel) for their butter and eggs. This shows how that "peculiar institution" of slavery develops a country. Had it been abolished years ago this would have been one of the most promising sections of the state. And yet the inhabitants are, like people of old, "joined to their idols", and opposed to emancipation.
    I am credibly informed, by one who is posted, that but eight Union men are to be found in the whole region. I hope after this rebellion is ended that some enterprising men of the North will settle here, and then the country will be so transfigured that the inhabitants would scarcely recognize it.
    Port Tobacco is but thirty-two miles from Washington, yet there is not such a thing as a saw mill nearer than Salisbury,

Somerset County, or the capital. Here's a chance for somebody. However, this is an important port, for a brick business was carried on with Dixie in spite of the blockade. If you will look at a map you will see an arm of the Potomac makes up toward Port Tobacco. This is called Port Tobacco River, though it is part of the Potomac. Port Tobacco was formerly at the head of navigation, but now the river at that place is not more than two feet deep and about twenty wide. What has caused it to change I do not know. About half a mile above this place is the head of navigation for sailing vessels, and the Point, which is 5 1/2 miles from Port Tobacco, is the last wharf for steamers. Yet neither here nor at the dock above is there anything more than a warehouse, while the wharves at both places are so rotten that a team cannot go upon them. A short distance below can be seen Mathias Point, once so celebrated, but now harmless; and in that neighborhood is our blockading squadron.

From Chapel Point, so named from the Chapel which adorns the head of the hill, went Sethson, who killed Lieut. White, of the 7th U.S. Colored Troops, a few weeks ago. Very few of the slaves in this region have gone into the army, no recruiting station or posts having been nearer than Benedict, about 40 miles below. Nearly all the inhabitants are Catholics, there being two churches of that faith in the vicinity — the one before spoken of, the other at Port Tobacco. Besides this there is an Episcopal Church, the pastor of which is a strong Union man. Previous to the war, his congregation numbered from 800 to 1000 members, but when the rebellion broke out he was requested to leave. He refused, saying "the church was as much his as anybody's." All his communicants left him but four. He still persisted in his Union sentiments, and when the Secretary of War heard of his case he sent the old pastor a Chaplain's commission, and he still preaches in the old pulpit. He is nearly eighty years old. All honor to such men say I.

We are awaiting orders and are still unsettled. Occasionally a paper makes its way into camp, (generally a week old) and is eagerly perused by all before it is destroyed. We have but six companies of the Legion at this point, two others being on the Pautuxent, and the others at Annapolis.

We have had some cold weather and this morning the ground was white with frost. Nuts and persimmons are plenty, and partridges, squirrels and rabbits are seen in camp (dead of course) very often. The trees, with the exception of the evergreens, are entirely denuded of leaves, and the landscape presents a dreary view.

Yours,

S.H.B., Jr.

Poughkeepsie Daily Eagle

[NEUTRAL IN NOTHING.]

Headquarters, Purnell Legion Md. Vols., Chapel Point, Md.
Dec. 18, 1863

Dear Eagle:

    We have had a visit from an anxiously-waited-for personage, the paymaster. A few more days and four months pay would have been due us.

    I took a ride last week to two of our detachments. My journey took me through a fine country, but unimproved; houses old and dilapidated, fences broken and in places torn down, and roads and bridges in bad condition. I remarked one peculiarity, a large number of gates across the public roads. Every farmer at the beginning and end of his farm throws a gate across the road to mark the extent of his possessions and save fences. We passed through several so called towns and villages. A store at the junction of two roads is considered a village. The largest one was called Newburg, and consisted of one store, one blacksmith shop, and two dwelling houses, the post office being in the store. Not much like our thriving neighbor of the same name on the Hudson.

    The principal crop is tobacco, which is raised in great abundance and of good quality. The livestock raised is generally horses and negroes, the number of both determining the wealth of the inhabitants. Very few of the poorer class of whites are found here, the county being the home of the negro aristocracy of the state.

I stopped all night with one of our detachments at a place called Lancaster Wharf. It is the principal wharf in this neighborhood, a steamer from Baltimore and Washington stopping on each trip. The night I stayed there some of our picket squad under Lieut. Christopher captured a man from the Virginia side of the Potomac. They failed to capture the boat, a small one, which with its crew immediately put back and probably reached Dixie in safety. The prisoner, whose name is Coskeny, claimed to be a British subject trying to get to Peoria, Illinois. He had on his person a certificate of naturalization and a passport from the consul at Richmond. He had been residing in Augusta, Georgia and had been seven weeks getting to the rebel capital. We detained him until we received orders from headquarters, and then sent him on his way rejoicing.

Since then three more have been captured, together with the boat — all refugees. One of them was a lady, who declared she was tired of rebeldom and never wished to return. They took the Oath of Allegiance, and were discharged. They did not care anything for the loss of the boat as long as they were on Union soil.

Wishing you a happy New Year,

I am yours, &c.

S.H.B., Jr.

𝔓𝔬𝔲𝔤𝔥𝔨𝔢𝔢𝔭𝔰𝔦𝔢 𝔇𝔞𝔦𝔩𝔶 𝔈𝔞𝔤𝔩𝔢

[NEUTRAL IN NOTHING.]

Headquarters, Purnell Legion Md. Vols.
Chapel Point, Md.
Jan. 24, 1864

Dear Eagle:

Though the phrase, "All quiet along the Potomac," has become a stereotyped one since the beginning of this war, yet I will have to repeat it regarding the section of river under our control. In fact, nothing has occurred to disturb or interrupt the monotony of our duties since my last.

The weather is a fertile subject to discuss, but even that has been so like that at the north that I can make nothing new out of it. We have had snow and ice — so have you. Although it has not been cold enough to freeze anybody, still it has been inclement enough to cause us to hug our stoves and use our overcoats. At present, however, it is quite warm and the ice has almost entirely disappeared from the river. I witnessed the breaking up in the Potomac near the mouth of Aquia Creek the other day. It was a magnificent sight, beyond the feeble powers of my pen to describe.

The gunboats occasionally amuse themselves by shelling the predatory bands of rebel cavalry that make their appearance near Mathias Point. It is about all they can do, for the blockade runners generally come and go in small boats that cannot be reached by large vessels. Most of them are loaded solely by refugees. I visited one of the detachments a few days ago and found a house full of them. The Baltimore and Washington boats had been unable to make their usual trips on account of the ice and these persons had accumulated on our hands. They were both black and white, and in a state of destitution, very glad to once more be in a land where they could live. Two, however, were genuine blockade runners who had been captured while engaged in their nefarious occupation and were, together with their goods, held subject to orders. The principal portion of their stock consisted of tobacco.

Considerable business in the way of recruiting negroes has been done in this part of the country under the auspices of Gen. Birney. It went very much against the grain of the slaveholders, most of them receiving a portion of the benefits of holding property that would take to its legs and run away.

We have had considerable trouble with squads of cavalry from Glasboro Point who visit this section. They are mounted patrols who are sent out to scour the country, and although under the charge of commissioned officers, think they have a license to pillage and destroy property, both public and private. I am ashamed to say that they are New York regiments; such men hurt the cause in which they are engaged by laying a foundation for the reports set in circulation by the copperheads.

The steamer General Meigs, bound for this place, was a few days since sunk near Baltimore. There was one error in the published accounts; instead of powder it was our provisions, clothing and stationary which were lost. Fortunately for us, we have on hand rations enough to last till the end of the month; otherwise there would be suffering among us.

Although politics fills the papers, that does not trouble us much. As the political parties at home will not allow us to vote, why should we care who is the next president? The great majority of the Democratic party don't want the soldiers to vote; the result of last autumn's vote among the soldiers that were allowed the elective franchise must convince the sympathizers of the rebels how the soldiers stand politically.

Many of the men in the Legion are reenlisting and probably the majority will do so before the time is up for the bounty for veterans. A furlough has also many charms for our men. The Port Tobacco Times contains this week quite a puff for our good behavior while here. This is gratifying, coming from a secessionist.

Yours & c,
S.H.B., Jr.

Poughkeepsie Daily Eagle

[NEUTRAL IN NOTHING.]

Headquarters, Purnell Legion, Md. Vols., Chapel Point, Md., April 12, 1864

Dear Eagle:

'Tis a long time since I indited a letter to you. The "Old Maryland Line" has declared for freedom. The election that took place in this state on Tuesday last was a memorable one in her annals. She shook herself loose from the grasp of the "old man of the sea," and stood boldly forth as one of the free states. Although the vote was not as large as expected, still it was decisive. In this district of Charles county but three votes were cast for the Convention, and in the county but thirteen votes were polled in the affirmative. Even the so called Union men could not relinquish their interest (as they called slavery) for their principles. And these people are a sample of the lower counties of Maryland. They are "joined to their idols," but will not be let alone by the progressive spirit of this age.

For several weeks the weather has been stormy and the tides unusually high. The farmers have been unable to do much in the way of farming. Last week a steamer came to the wharf on board of which were several officers and colored soldiers, who were on a recruiting tour. They succeeded very well — getting more recruits than I expected; nearly all the able bodied negroes have left this neighborhood. It was quite amusing to see the party on their journey; as they marched through the country they sang in concert, led by the officer who had them in charge, "John Brown's body lies mouldering in the grave." I thought if the old man's spirit was looking upon the scene, he must have felt that his martyrdom was useful and glorious.

Sunday was a busy and ludicrous scene when the boat bringing back our men arrived at the wharf. Female blacks of all sizes and ages thronged the wharf, waiting for a chance to get away from thralldom. Here you would see a sprightly mulatto girl with a bright handkerchief tied around her head — turban fashion, carrying all her possessions in a small bundle; and there you would see an elderly woman, black as midnight, "toting" in her arms a heavy baby, while following were numerous others of all shades of color.

Two things have struck me as singular during my sojourn south. First, the infantile age at which the young blacks become strong enough to walk; and second, the numerous mulatto and quadroon children which the slave women give birth to.

This country possesses many curiosities for the antiquarian. Our Quartermaster had presented to him while in town one day, a book containing the laws of Henry VII and Henry VIII, printed in Old English and published in 1720. It had been originally bound in calf, but time and vermin had destroyed the greater part of the covers. The print was legible and bold. I have in my possession manuscripts of the same year, but written in this country.

In the graveyard there is a grave, judging from the stone which covers it, nearly 160 years old. The stone, which was brought from England, was originally in the shape of a cross and is freestone. I took a sketch of it today with its inscription, the latter of which I append: "Here lyes the body of Elizabeth, ye Daughter of Col. Henry Darnell,, by his Wife Mad'm Elinor Darnell. She was married to Mr. Edward Digges, ye 8th day of January, 1699, and departed this Life ye 9th day of May, 1705. May She now Enjoy Eternal Bliss. Amen." Much skill is displayed in the finish of the stone, and probably at the time its manufacture and purchase it was considered extravagant.

  The chapel on the hill, from which this Point derives its name, is of ancient origin, although an addition has been put to it within the last twenty years. It would pay him who proposes writing a history of this war to journey through this country.
Yours & c.
S.H.B., Jr.

{Most of our readers are probably aware that the little word "ye," in the above inscription, was substituted for "the" when the "Old English" or "Black Letter" was in vogue. The th, which were cast together, like fl, ff, etc., so closely resembled the y, that the latter character was often used in spelling the definite article.}

𝔓𝔬𝔲𝔤𝔥𝔨𝔢𝔢𝔭𝔰𝔦𝔢 𝔇𝔞𝔦𝔩𝔶 𝔈𝔞𝔤𝔩𝔢

[NEUTRAL IN NOTHING.]

Head Q'rs Purnell Leg'n, Md. Vols., Somewhere in Virginia, June 6, 1864

Dear Eagle:

We left Chapel Point on the 18th of May, and have been with the Army of the Potomac since the 21st ult. General Lockwood brought us from Belle Plain to the Fifth Corps. On the 29th ult. We were assigned to the Third Brigade, Second Division, and on the 30th, about 4 P.M., we went into action. We were, with the rest of the brigade, put on the extreme left of the line, and had nothing to do but drive in the rebel skirmish line, which we did effectively, having but four men wounded. We were under fire for three and a half hours, having gone into action at four P.M., and coming out about half-past seven.

The next day a portion of the Regiment was sent out on the skirmish line, but the Rebs retired. All night heavy firing was heard on the right and the Brigade was ordered up as support. During the night we changed our position and threw up breastworks, and that is the plan we have had to adopt ever since we came here. We advance and throw up temporary entrenchments and throw out our skirmishers. On the 3d of this month the Regiment was put out on the skirmish line with orders to drive the rebels out of their rifle pits, which we did, capturing from 20 to 25 Johnnies, but losing in the affair eight men killed and twenty-one wounded. A portion of the latter, however, were slightly wounded and are now fit for duty.

The rebels shelled the woods in which we were stationed, but injured but very few men. They have a battery of six pieces called the "Richmond Battery" — five of the guns are 24 pounders. It is the only battery (I have been credibly informed) that we have been unable to silence, but I think we shall get it after a while.

Last night, just after dark, we changed our position very silently, but owing to the noise made by some of the Regiments the Johnnies discovered that we were moving and made a heavy attack on our skirmish line, driving them inside the breastworks. Fortunately for us we were ahead of them in a ravine and did not get much of the fire. We are now at Headquarters of the Corps, which is commanded by Major General Warren, my old Colonel. Our Brigade is called the Maryland Brigade and commanded by Colonel Dushane of the First Maryland Volunteers, a brave man and much liked by all who know him. His Assistant Adjutant General was captured about a week ago while outside the pickets and we have thus far lost about forty men in killed and wounded.

There is heavy firing every day and night somewhere in the Army, judging from the sound, but we can learn nothing of the actions except from rumors, which are not always reliable. I have not seen a paper later than the 21st of May. Some of the prisoners have had Richmond papers of the 24th, but the only news of importance was the acknowledgment of a reverse. My address is Third Brigade, Second Division, Fifth Army Corps, via Washington, D.C.

Yours in haste,
S.H.B., Jr.

Poughkeepsie Daily Eagle

[NEUTRAL IN NOTHING.]

Kirkwood House, Washington, D.C.
January 10, 1865

Dear Eagle:
    Thinking that you might be pleased to get a letter from me. I have taken advantage of a rainy day to indite the following: I drifted here last Saturday morning and found as usual, after a rain, Washington a mud hole. However the sun made his appearance in a few hours and we had our usual rations of dust. This city has been so often described by abler writers than I, so that will be a forbidden subject for me. Suffice it to say that it is the same "city of magnificent distances."
    A large number of officers and soldiers are to be seen in the city streets, hotels and places of amusements; but I am informed by a person who is (or seems to be) well posted, that the number is not as large as usual. Very many of the former are not exactly in the service, but are here settling their accounts that they may receive their final pay.
    The city is overrun by civilians who have flocked here as usual to look after the interests of the nation. The meetings of the "third house" are numerous and well attended by these patriots, most of whom seem to be well supplied with "greenbacks."
    I had the pleasure yesterday of hearing a portion of the debate in the House of Representatives on the "Amendment to the Constitution." The speech of Mr. Odell was a most eloquent oration and, coming as it did of a former prominent member of

the Democratic Party. It was an important straw showing the direction of the wind. Several members of that party are trying to get rid of the incubus that has heretofore borne down that and all other political parties, so to begin the year 1865 right.

I was not aware of the debate in the Senate, or I should have tried to hear a part of it at least. The attendance at the lower House was not as large as I expected for the importance of the question. But the fact is nearly everybody is tired of the oft repeated arguments in defence of slavery and care not to hear them. The places of amusement seem to be well attended and no stranger would think from the appearance of the people everywhere that war, cruel, deadly, civil war was in the land.

The ladies of this city are as gay and showy as ever, but I must be so ungallant to them as to say they are not as beautiful as I had a reason to expect. Like every city there are beauties and belles; but I think Main Street on a fine summer's eve can show as fine a procession of handsome ladies. But more dress is displayed than at home, particularly by strangers. However, not being a critic of that article I will attempt no description of the prevailing styles.

A large number of railroad accidents have taken place within the last fortnight on railroads running to this place, but I was fortunate enough to escape them. Recruiting goes on quite fast here and I hear, or was told rather, that no draft will be necessary. Among the numerous visitors are several of the officers who escaped from rebel hands within the last month. Of course they prefer the change.

Major Leslie who came here with me left on Saturday afternoon to rejoin his regiment. Large numbers of officers are coming north on leaves of absence. As I know of little news and the newspapers publish the speeches delivered, I will close.
Yours & c.,
S.H.B., Jr.

Poughkeepsie Eagle July 3, 1865

Capt. Stephen H. Bogardus, Jr. of this city, has lately been the recipient of two handsome swords, presents, one from a comrade in arms and the other from the men of his company. The first is a regulation sword, steel scabbard, mounted for service, with the inscription: "Presented to Capt. Stephen H. Bogardus, Jr. of Co. E, 192 Regt. N.Y.S.V., by Lieut. E.F. Foster, late Q.M. of Purnell Legion, Maryland Vols., April 1, 1865."

The other is an elegant sword, with handsomely ornamented hilt, engraved blade, gold plated scabbard, and very heavy sword knot. It was made by Tiffany & Co., N.Y. and cost $500. It is inscribed: "Presented to Capt. Stephen H. Bogardus, Jr., by the members of Co. E, 192d Regt., N.Y.S.V., May 10, 1865."

Index

1

111th Pennsylvania
  Volunteers 44
124th Pennsylvania
  Volunteers 59
14th Louisiana Volunteers
  (CSA) 41
14th New Jersey Volunteers .. 64
150th New York Volunteers .. 64
192nd New York Volunteers ......
  .... XV, 94
1st District of Columbia
  Volunteers 52
1st Eastern.Shore Maryland.
  Regiment 69
1st Maryland 14, 43, 91
1st Maryland Cavalry 67

2

20th New York State Militia
  .... 8, 72
20th New York Volunteers
  (Turner Rifles) 25
21st Indiana Volunteers 12, 14
21st North Carolina State
  Troops (CSA) 46
24th Virginia Volunteers
  (CSA) 41
28th Virginia Volunteers
  (CSA) 41
2nd Delaware Volunteers 14

3

3rd Delaware Volunteers 64

4

4th Wisconsin Volunteers 14

5

5th New York Volunteers
see (Duryée Zouaves)
5th North Carolina State
  Troops (CSA) 41

6

6th Michigan Volunteers 14
60th New York Volunteers
  .... 48, 52, 56

7

78th NewYork Volunteers 48
7th Maryland Volunteers 68
7th U.S. Colored Troops 80

9

9th New York State Militia 58

A

Accomac County, VA ... 16, 21
Alexandria, VA 54
Allen, A.L. 48
Army of the Potomac
  .... 77, 78, 90
Annapolis, MD 69, 72
Antietam, MD ....
  .... 63, 64, 71, 74, 75
Aquia Creek, VA 84
Arctic (Steamer) 35
Atkins, Alfred 1, 2, 6
Augusta, GA 83

B

"Baby Waker" 44
Baltimore American 66

Baltimore, MD............2, 7, 8, 9, 10, 12, 25, 26, 28, 32, 39, 40, 41, 53, 64, 66, 79, 83, 85
Banks, Gen. Nathaniel 49, 56, 57
Bartlett, Lt. Col. Charles......64
Beauregard, Gen. P.G.T........50
Bel Haven, VA........................23
Belle Island, VA......................74
Belle Plain, VA.......................90
Belvedere (Steamer)....................10
Benedict................................80
Berryville, VA.........................49
Big Bethel, VA.......................29
Bird's Nest.............................23
Birney, Gen. David B...........85
Blue Ridge, VA..........48, 50, 53
Bolivar Heights, VA.......43, 61
Boonsboro, MD......................71
Boyle, Capt............................45
Brandywine Creek..................74
Brinckerhoff, Daniel................1
Brouner, Lt. Richard..............68
Brown, John.......................61, 87
Buasing, John........................27
Bull Run, VA..........................9

C

Cambridge, NY......................47
Camp Bay View, VA.......32, 37
Camp Goodrich, VA 44, 49, 52
Camp Hamilton, VA.........5, 28
Camp Monocacy, MD.........71
Camp Van Buren, VA..........40
Cape Hatteras........................27
Cedar Creek, VA....................50
Chapel Point, MD..........79, 80, 82, 84, 87, 90

Charles County, MD............87
Charlestown, WV....................61
Cherry Stone Inlet...........24, 31
Chesapeake Bay.......................31
Christopher, Lt........................83
City Hotel..............................71
City of Glasgow..............................35
Company Q............................78
Cooper, Gen............................52
Coskeny.................................83
Courtenir, Lt. Charles...........29
Cumberland............................71
Curtin, Gov. Andrew.............77

D

Darnell, Elinor.........................88
Darnell, Henry........................88
Davis, Henry Winter.............77
Davis, Jefferson......................67
Digges, Edward.....................88
Dix, Gen. John..........10, 15, 31
Doughty, Mrs..........................39
Doughty, William..................38
Druid Hill Park, MD.............59
Drummondtown, VA 19, 20, 21, 24, 37
Dunkard Church.....................72
Duryee's Zouaves (5th New York Volunteers).............1, 5, 8, 13, 14, 17, 27, 29, 48, 121
Dushane, Col..........................91

E

Eastville, VA.............23, 24, 26, 28, 29, 30, 31, 33
Express (Tug Boat)................29

F

Fallkill Creek, NY..................14

Fanning 6
Farquair County, VA 54
Federal Hill, MD .... ix, 2, 4,
    7, 8, 10, 12, 25, 27
Fire Zouaves 48
First Maryland 14, 81, 91
Five Points 41
Floyd, John B. 35
Fort Delaware, MD 74, 77
Fort McHenry 26
Fort Monroe, VA 28
Fort Schuyler, NY 1
Fort Sumter, SC 41
Foster, Lt. E.F. 94
Francktown, VA 23
Frederick, MD 63, 66, 68,
    69, 70
Fremont, Gen. John C. 49
Front Royal, VA 50, 52, 53
Fulton, Capt. 31

G

General Meigs (Steamer) ... 85
Georgianna (Steamer) 28
George Washington (Steamer) 29
Glasboro Point 85
Gordonsville, VA 54

H

Hagerstown, MD 67
Hamblin, Capt. Joseph 5
Harper's Ferry, VA 42, 43,
    48, 50, 56, 57, 61, 64, 67, 68,
    69
Haskins, Maj. 27
Hedgeman's River 57
Hercules (Steamer) 13
Hog Island, VA 37, 38
Hooker, Gen. Joseph 59

Hudson River, NY 4, 82
Hull, Maj. Harmon 26

I

Irish Brigade 72

J

Jackson, Gen. Thomas J.
    (Stonewall) 43, 47, 49,
    50, 57
Jefferson 70
Johannes, Col. John G. ..... x, 18
Johnston, Gen. Jospeh E.
    .... 43, 44

K

Kadysville (sic) Keedysville,
    MD 59
Kanawha, VA 35
Keedysville, MD 72
Kenly, Col. John 46
King's Creek 31
Kirkwood House 92
Knoxville 69

L

Lancaster Wharf 83
Lee, Byron 47
Leslie, Maj. 93
Lester, G. Edward 78
Little Washington 57
Lockwood, Gen. H.H.
    .... 18, 25, 31, 32, 90
Locust Point 10
Lossing, Benson J. 66
Loudon County, VA 64
Loudon Heights, VA 69

M

Main Street, Poughkeepsie, NY 93
Manassas, VA 50, 66
Manassas Gap, VA 50
Mary Powell 60
Maryland Battalion 43
Maryland Blast Works 4
Maryland Heights, MD 44, 68
Mathias Point, VA 80, 84
McClellan, Gen. George B. 8, 57
McDowell, Gen. Irvin 49
Meade, Gen. George 78
Meigs, Gen. Montgomery ... 85
Meridan, VA 52
Merrimac 40, 59
Micawber 63
Middletown, VA 49, 52
Milroy, Gen. Robert H. 49
Modesttown, VA 19, 20
Monocacy Junction, MD 64
Monumental City (Baltimore), MD 2, 8, 14, 28, 42
Mulligan, Col. James 5

N

Newburg 82
Newport News, VA 29
Newtown, MD 12, 14, 16
Norfolk, VA 40
North Branch 50
North Point lighthouse 35
North River 28, 50
Northampton County, VA 23, 24, 30, 31, 33

Nun's Battery 14

O

Oakhill, VA 16
Odell, Mr. 92

P

Pacific (Steamer) 35
Paddock, Chaplain 75
Pangoteague 37
Patapsco River 4
Patterson, Capt. 32
Pautuxent 81
Pea Ridge, AK 49
Peoria, IL 83
Pierce, Gen. Ebenezer 29
Pierpont, Gov. Francis 35
Pittsburgh, TN 41
Pleasant Valley, NY 14
Ploss 72
Pocahontas (Steamer) 12, 13
Pocomoke Sound 13
Pocomoke River 14
Point Lookout, MD 78
Pollock, Irving B. 72
Pope, Gen. John 54
Port Tobacco Times 86
Port Tobacco, MD 79, 80
Potomac River 50, 69, 77, 78, 80, 83, 84, 90
Potts, Dr. J.G. 37, 38
Pougateague 25, 26
Poughkeepsie Boys 1, 2, 22
Poughkeepsie, NY .... , 2, 6, 8, 9, 22
Purnell Legion 14, 18, 27, 30, 33, 39, 63, 66, 68, 71, 74, 77, 79, 82, 84, 87, 90, 120

R

Rappahannock River, VA 53, 67
Ray, Chaplain 75
Reading Cavalry 14
Red Devils (Duryee's Zouaves) 2, 16
Red, White and Blue 25
Reynold's U.S. Battery 44
Richmond Battery (CSA) ..91
Richmond, VA 50, 57, 58, 76, 83, 91
Rosecrans, Gen. William S. 77
Rush's Lancers 64

S

Salisbury 79
Sanitary Commission 58
Schenk, Gen. Robert 64
Schoepf, Gen. Albin 75
Sethson 80
Sewell's Point 29
Sharpsburg, MD 73
Shenandoah River, VA ...., 49, 50, 69
Shields, Gen. James 49
Sigel, Gen. Franz 49
Simpson, Maj 44
Slough, Col. John 48, 49
Smith, A.B. 6
Smith, Col. 24
Snicker's Ferry 49
Somerset County 80
Sons of Malta 5
Star (Steamer) 26
South Mountain, MD 57, 63
Star Spangled Banner ...12, 25
Steamer Geo. Washington..29

Strasburg, VA 49, 50
Strasburg and Front Royal Railroad 50

T

Talt, Col. 52
Tappan Zee, NY 4
Temperanceville, VA 19, 20, 24
Tiffany & Co. 94
Townfields, VA 31, 37
Tuthill, Dr. Robert K. 9
Tyndell, Joseph 6

U

United States Hotel 63, 71, 72

V

Vallandigham, Hon. Clement 75
Van Wagner, James 1

W

Warren, Gen. G.K. 8, 25, 91
Warrenton Whig 58
Warrenton, VA ...52, 54, 56, 58
Washington, D.C. 62, 79, 83, 85, 91, 92
Washington, VA 53
Washington County, NY 47
Waterloo, VA 56
Watkins, Lt. 37
Westchester County, NY 27
Westminister, MD 5, 9
White, Lt. 80
White's Independent Cavalry 64

Williamsport 41
Wilmington, DE 75
Wilson's Branch, VA 23
Winchester Republican 48
Winchester, VA
.... 45, 46, 49, 53, 67
Wise, Henry 19
Wood, Gov. Fernando 67

Y

Yankee Doodle 23

Z

Zous Zous (Zouaves) 2, 25
Zouaves 1, 5, 8, 13, 14, 17, 27, 29, 48

About the Editor

Joel Craig has been a Civil War historian since the age of 10. Currently, he is president of The Ulster County Civil War Round Table; A member of *Company A, 5th NY Duryee Zouaves*; and a member of the *Company of Military Historians*.

Brian Pohanka

Brian C. Pohanka is a military historian, author, lecturer and consultant who has devoted many years to the study of 19th and early 20th century military history, with emphasis on the American Civil War and the battle of Little Bighorn. He was a senior researcher, writer and advisor on all of Time-Life Books Civil War projects, and was Series Consultant for the A&E/History Channel television documentary *Civil War Journal*.

In addition to his frequent lectures and appearances in television documentaries and independent video productions, he served as an historical advisor and military coordinator for a number of films, including *Glory* (for which he recruited and instructed a company of soldiers for the 54th Massachusetts), *Gettysburg, Gods and Generals* and *Cold Mountain*.. He is the author of *Distant Thunder: A Photographic Essay on the Civil War, The Civil War: An Aerial Portrait, Landscapes of the Civil War*, Don Troiani's *Civil War Art*, and co-author of *Mapping the Civil War, Custer's Field* and *Myles Keogh: An Irish Dragoon in the 7th Cavalry*. He participates in Civil War living history as Captain of Company A, 5th New York Volunteer Infantry, Duryée's Zouaves.

www.ingramcontent.com/pod-product-compliance
Lightning Source LLC
Chambersburg PA
CBHW022304060426
42446CB00007BA/588